Matriliny among the Khasis

Matriliny among the Khasis

A Study in Retrospect and Prospect

M. Sasikumar

Published, 2019

Published by

Gyan Publishing House
5, Ansari Road
Daryaganj, New Delhi-110002
Phone: 011-47034999, 9811692060
www.gyanbooks.com
E-mail: books@gyanbooks.com

and

Anthropoligical Survey of India
27 Jawaharlal Nehru Road,
Kolkata - 700016, (West Bengal)
Tel.: (033) 22521698
www. ansi.gov.in

Printed at: G. Print Process, Delhi.

Cataloging in Publication Data—DK
Courtesy: D.K. Agencies (P) Ltd. <docinfo@dkagencies.com>

Sasikumar, M. *(Anthropologist)*, **author.**
Matriliny among the Khasis : a study in retrospect and prospect / by M. Sasikumar.
pages cm
Study conducted in Nongkrem and Sawmer villages of East Khasi Hills District, Meghalaya, India.
Includes bibliographical references.
ISBN 9788121217538

1. Khasi (Indic people)—India—Nongkrem—Kinship. 2. Khasi (Indic people)—India—Sawmer—Kinship. 3. Matrilineal kinship—India—Nongkrem. 4. Matrilineal kinship—India—Sawmer. I. Title.

LCC DS432.K5S27 2019 | DDC 306.83 23

Contents

Contents

Foreword

Kinship study is the crown of anthropology. It is to anthropology what the study of state is to political science. Kinship relations are universally found, notwithstanding the scale of society, although in contemporary times, it may not be the principle of social organization as Lewis H. Morgan thought.

The ubiquity of kinship is because each society has bonds of consanguinity and affinity – the kinspersons share biogenetic substances, though adoption of children in a group from the other groups may also be practiced, and persons conquered as slaves from neighbouring communities may also be adopted in a family in course of time depending upon their good demeanour. At the same time, irrespective of the wide-ranging forms of sexuality (such as live-in relations, same sex marriages and sharing, multiple sexual deeds, divorces and remarriages, mannequins serving as partners), heterosexual unions, of enduring variety, with children being born to these, are equally universal. Change is a permanent feature of all institutions, customs and practices, groups and communities. Kinship systems have also changed and are continuously changing; but it is far from being true that they have disappeared or relegated to insignificance.

Kinship studies were central to anthropological researches in the mid-twentieth century, and later, for a few decades. One cannot think of a British anthropologist of that time who did not contribute to a sophisticated understanding of the kinship system of the society he or she studied. The animated debates – sometimes dovetailing with interpersonal animosity– between 'descent' and 'alliance' theorists, the folklore of which is still alive in British universities, richly contributed to the anthropological grasp of 'kinship relations in society'. However, as time rolled by, kinship studies witnessed their fast replacement in the studies of economy and development, displacement and resettlement, formal organizations, professions and markets, migration and transformation of cities, revolts and movements, ethno-medicine, social stratification, and many other sub-interests assumed to be sought by the grotesquely expanding market. Kinship was left out as a field of research without a modicum of realisation that if there is any institution that the anthropologists exclusively study, it is kinship. For the study of other institutions, such as economy, polity, and religion, and processes (such as socialisation), we often need inputs from sister disciplines that undertake a specialised study of these institutions and processes, like economics, political science, philosophy and theology, linguistics, and psychology.

Against this backdrop, it is heartening to note M. Sasikumar's book on matrilineal kinship, a comparative study of two communities, classically taught as examples of matrilineal societies, the Khasi and the Nair. Based on a first-hand fieldwork carried out with the members of both these communities, the author of this book is comparatively more privileged than the others, for he shares his consanguinity with the community of the Nair of Kerala. However, the autobiographical input, used rather sparingly, has been closely sieved through the lens of objectivity, so unless told, the reader would fail to know that this book's author has an insider's understanding of one of the matrilineal communities because of the fact of being raised in it. Objectivity triumphs over any subjective collapse, which is quite likely in an auto-ethnographic account.

Sasikumar keeps pace with time. He is aware of the moment in the history of anthropology when oddities of the communities were recorded, as juicily as possible, to bring home the enormous diversity of human living and also, to shock, alert, befuddle, or surprise the western public with the cultural manners and artefacts of the non-western world. Certainly, the customs and practices, beliefs and rituals, and thoughts and actions that were documented with elaborate details, were not the figments of imagination, although the description, and the language used for this, might have given this impression, the point, which unabashedly was missed out, was that they were incessantly changing, in some cases gradually, in others briskly.

Moreover, as Claude Lévi-Strauss earlier noted, when anthropologists embarked on the study of these societies, they were already considerably 'mutilated', to use his expression, because of the onslaught of colonialism in their contexts; they were neither 'frozen rivers' nor 'fixed exhibits'. It was expected that their ethnographers would keep in their respective perspectives the element of time, the idea that all systems and ways of living are perennially transformable, but so committed were they to the notion of 'uniqueness' that they constructed the system as it was, or as it was thought to be, with the tacit assumption that it would continue to be what it is now in future as well. In other words, the conflation was of 'what it was in the past', a piece of knowledge largely collected by interviewing people and the reading of travel accounts, and 'what it is', for which the technique of observation was used. The construction of the system thus reached was communicated to the wider world through the pages of ethnography, studded with pictures of the people and their activities, which had a longer life than the institution itself, with the result that the Nair came to be etched in mind as the bastion of a natolocal residence, and the Khasi men as suffering from a feeling of lowliness.

In his book, Sasikumar explodes these images, showing aptly that the encroachment of economic frontiers has made these systems, which looked unique at one time, resemble that of their neighbours. An expansion of opportunities, surfacing with urban-industrialization, hastened the process of occupational diversification and mobility of people, their geographical passages, and the rise of individualism, as a consequence of which the hitherto tradition-bound persons were liberated from the shackles of what they thought were the 'oppressive rules and conducts'. Matrilineal societies, Sasikumar submits, resulted from a combination of social and historical factors; for instance, the Nair system required, on one hand, its men to be warriors, being away from home serving the South Indian principalities, on the other, a particular custom of marriage among the Nambudiri Brahmin, where only the eldest brother was permitted to marry, and the rest be consigned to bachelorhood, who would have the relations of *sambandham* with Nair women. As the polity changed, no more were men needed as warriors. Instead, they could pursue higher education, get into white-collar jobs, move out of their traditional homesteads and start a nuclear family, with egalitarian conjugal relations, and if possible, a bilineal descent. Sasikumar's work looks into these external forces that impinge upon the internal, and change the society to bear semblance, at least apparent, with the 'global society'.

Matrilineal societies always puzzled the anthropologists, for the issue these societies faced was of combining matrilineal descent, matriarchy (authority in the hands of women), and matrilocality (residence sponsored by the mother); and this problem which Audrey Richards called 'matrilineal puzzle' necessitated certain solutions, which varied from one matrilineal society to another. The crux lay in the ethnographic observation (generally called the 'third principle of kinship' in Robin Fox's work) that men usually exercise control, at least till now, in all societies, so women may be the owners of property, but men organise control over it. Therefore, matrilineal societies are constrained to keep men (brothers, husbands) for political control as well as economic operations. It also explains the absence of matriarchy in matrilineal societies.

Sasikumar's close examination of matrilineal societies, with two detailed case studies, suggests the perpetual instability of matrilineal societies. The situation of equilibrium that the anthropologists had earlier noted in these societies was not only temporary but also at the surface level. Underneath were the currents of keeping contradictory forces together, which later became the prime mover of change. When 'matrilineal men' came in contact with the contiguously-situated patrilineal people, they felt 'diminished in their manhood', so said Patricia Mukhim, the Padma Shri awardee from Meghalaya, and it was enough to intensify the simmering which already was there because of the dissatisfaction that the members of a gender category had as a consequence of being excluded from the descent group. By examining the matrilineal society against the backdrop of the exteriorly-induced changes and inner dynamics, Sasikumar's work is a significant contribution to kinship studies, a field that should not remain ignored in the discipline of anthropology.

Vinay Kumar Srivastava

Acknowledgements

I am grateful to the Director, Anthropological Survey of India, for accepting my research proposal and giving me an opportunity to undertake the present study. Many people helped me at different stages of conception, formulation and implementation of this project. Prof. Vinay Kumar Srivastava, the present Director of Anthropological Survey of India, is a constant source of encouragement and support. If he has not been seen this repot it would not have been seen the day light. He has gone through the report word by word and suggested changes which enhanced the quality of the report to a great extent. Thanks are due to Dr. Ramesh Chandra, then Deputy Director and Dr. B. Francis Kulirani, then Superintending Anthropologist and Head of Office, Anthropological Survey of India, North East Regional Centre, Shillong for their constant encouragement and support. I am grateful to my senior colleagues Dr. Rajendra Prasad Athparia, Dr. Biibhash Dhar and Dr. Rip Roshina Gowloog at Anthropological Survey of India, Shillong. They never spared any occasion to help me in different ways in the successful completion of this study. I am grateful to Mrs Rosily Francis, Statistician, Dr. R. Senkuttuvan, Assistant Linguist, Dr. Sumit Mukherjee, Cartographer, and Shri. Ramesh Sahani, Assistant Anthropologist and Smt. Bandana Das, Research Associate, for their help and support. Mr Sukanta Saha, Sound Technician at NERC, was of immense help in preparing tables and charts.

In the field many people helped me to establish rapport with the informants. Bah B. Lyngdoh, the then officiating Lyngdoh at the Court of Syiem of Smit of Nongkrem was of immense help to me. I thank him for all the help he extended to me to feel comfortable in the field and for the wealth of information he shared. I am also very thankful to Bah. A.L. Shabong the Secretay of the Sawmer village. I am extremely thankful to Mr Hercules Kharbuli and Mr Gilbert Thankiew my field guides and my colleague Mr. Rani for introducing me to the secretary of the Sawmer village.

Last but not least I am very thankful to all my Khasi informants. If they have not shared the information with me this study would not have been possible. I sincerely thank each and every one of them.

M. Sasikumar

Preface

The people of India have a variety of kinship systems and they can be broadly categorised into three types; patrilineal, matrilineal, and bilineal. Barring two important pockets of people following matrilineal systems in the south-west and north-east part of India, the rest of Indian population is predominantly patrilineal. People following bilateral systems, with both parents being relevant for reckoning kinship and for claiming rights to resources are comparatively few in Indian population. There are also communities which reckon descent matrilineally but follow patrilineal mode of inheritance and succession patterns. The communities having matrilineal social systems exhibit no uniform matrilineal structure and differ from one community to another, and even among different subgroups of the same community. Structurally, the matrilineal societies differ from patrilineal ones in a number of significant areas such as inheritance, succession, residence, gender relations and customs and practices.

Women in matrilineal societies are seen as empowered to face the challenges of innovations compared to their counterparts in patrilineal societies. But no matrilineal society, atleast in India, can be found where women enjoy absolute authority and power. There is a general notion that all the matrilineal societies are matriarchal as well. But matriliny and matriarchy are not synonymous. Matriarchy implies the dominance of women in decision making. Authority is vested in her, both in theory and in practise. She is the channel not merely for inheritance, but also for succession to positions of authority in the family. Bachofen's theory that matriliny (descent through women) and matriarchy (rule by women) were but two aspects of the same institution is also disputable. From the perspective of cultural evolution, it is quite probable that the two aspects were combined. But, there are several instances where lineality is not necessarily associated with power.

Though matrilineal system was much more widely distributed in India, the matrilineal communities and the communities bearing matrilineal elements are chiefly found in the north-east and south-west parts of India. The Khasi of Meghalaya is an important tribal group who follow the matrilineal system in the north-east part of India. The Nair of Kerala was a classic example for matrilineal society in south India. Though both the Khasi and the Nair communities fall in the wider category of matrilineal societies they differ widely in its structure, function and components. Still a few parallels are observable. Differences are more than similarities.

The reasons for choosing to attempt a comparison of Khasi matrilineal system with that of Nair system were initially out of curiosity. The first exposure of the researcher to the Khasi society made him feel the steadfastness of the community in keeping the elements of matrilineal system as strictly as possible even though other aspects of their culture including the religion and belief systems had undergone drastic changes. The researcher was familiar with the factors which brought drastic changes in the Nair matrilineal system such as the impact of cash economy, western style education, improved communication facilities, British imposed and interpreted law on the complex social structure, etc. The eagerness was to understand how far these factors are present in the Khasi society and how it is operating and if it is evident in that society how the structural mechanism is resisting the changes. But the comparison did not limit only to Nairs and wherever the comparable data are available, has attempted to compare it with other matrilineal societies, like Kurichians of Kerala, Arumbukuttam Vellalas of Tamilnadu, Rabhas, Garos, etc.

Several extraneous elements are gradually penetrating in the social self of the Khasi community. Some elements like Christianity, with a strong patrilineal bias, have already made deep inroads in their socio-religious life. Those who embraced Christianity began to neglect many of their customs and practises and rites and rituals without observing them as strictly as earlier. Christianity often prefers the paternal to maternal involvements in their socio-religious observances. The modern transport and communication facilities have helped them to shift from traditional subsistence based agricultural productions to cash crops. This shift in their production pattern introduced them to a commercial economy bringing tremendous changes in their lifestyles. As a result, the little stratified Khasi society emerges as a stratified society based on property and income. A middle class based on economic prosperity is gradually emerging among them. In such a society negative sanctions by the community against the deviants seldom works and it ultimately affects the continuity of the matrilineal system itself.

Systematic studies are yet to be undertaken to understand the current problems peculiar to each such societies in the backdrop of matrilineal systems prevalent among them. The present study discusses the social systems of the Khasis in detail from both historical and present perspectives. It also tries to understand the structure of the role, power and function of both men and women in a social system where the position of women has been said to be more comfortable due to the matrilineal system.

M. Sasikumar

Chapter -1

Introduction

In anthropological literature matriliny is defined as the principle of reckoning descent through the mother or female line. Descent can be traced either matrilineally or patrilineally or bilaterally (i.e. either on female line or on male line or both). However only when such lines of descent are culturally recognised by a given community, that a particular community can be described as matrilineal or patrilineal or bilateral group. When female sex is the distinguishing criterion the descent principle or line is called matrilineal. The individuals' initial relationship is to their mother and through her to other kinsperson, both male and female, but continues only through females (Schneider and Gough, 1961:3). The descent principles may also influence the rules of inheritance, succession, locality and authority patterns of a community. The three interrelated concepts developed around the 'matri-complex' are matrilineal, matrilocal and matriarchal or matripotestal. Matrilineal refers to descent or inheritance or succession through women, matrilocal or uxorilocal denotes the residence of married couples after marriage with the wife's family or kin group and matriarchal indicates the authority of women. It is not an absolute necessity that a matrilineal community should also be matrilocal and matriarchal as well as far as residence and authority are concerned. In matrilineal societies residence is either duolocal or patrilocal or virilocal. Among the Nairs of Central Kerala residence was duolocal and among the Nairs of North Kerala it was patrilocal during the lifetime of husbands. Gould and Kolb (1964) state "matrilineal descent is found not only with matrilocal (uxorilocal) residence but also with patrilocal and virilocal residence" (Quoted in Chowdhury, 1978).

It was Bachofen who first posed matrilineal descent as a unique system in his book *Das Mutterrecht* (1861). He associated the evolution of matrilineal system with the invention of agriculture by women. Nineteenth century social scientists like McLennan, E.BTylor, and L.H.Morgan believed that matriliny existed prior to patriliny in the evolutionary ladder. Morgan holds that at the time when the one-sided exogamous group originated "marriage between single pairs was unknown and descent through males could not be traced with certainty". Hence he contended, in the archaic form of the kin group, kinship could be reckoned only through the maternal line, which also determined inheritance (Cited in Lowie, 1960:20). It has been theorised (Cf. Ehrenfels, 1941) that "mother right" was the original method of tracing biological descent, all over the world, for the obvious reason of the certainty of maternal identity. When the paternity of the children was assured, through monogamous marriages, descent in the female line was superimposed with the patrilineal system of descent. Engels opined that wherever group marriages exist, descent is traceable only on the maternal side, and thus the female line alone is recognised. For Morgan patriliny is quite a recent institution. Another evolutionist, E.B. Tylor, tried to explain the evolution of the system with much more empirical data. He categorised primitive tribes into three categories, those with a maternal system of descent, those in which both maternal and paternal rules of descent co-exist and those with a purely patrilineal descent. He argued that the institution of "couvade" (the custom, in many societies, for fathers to participate in the period of recuperation, after their wives give birth by remaining inactive for a long period of time- often much longer than the women) as the adjustmental mechanism in the process of transformation of societies from matriliny to patriliny. The twentieth-century anthropologists discarded their evolutionary mask and studied matrilineal kinship system "merely as particular examples of functionally integrated social structures" (Schneider and Gough, 1961).

Briffault (1927) observed that in highly developed agricultural societies, where plough cultivation dominates, the matrilineal form of society was generally absent. Where matrilineal culture is found among more developed communities they are usually located in high lands. Khasis, Garos, Jaintias and Rabhas are few examples. The Nairs of Kerala and Arumbukuttam Vellalas of Tamil Nadu were exceptional in having matrilineal system in a highly developed literate civilization, chiefly located in plains.

Matriliny and Matriarchy

Matriliny and matriarchy are not synonymous. There is a general belief that all the matrilineal societies are matriarchal as well. This is a myth created by earlier writers by the identical use of the terms matriliny and matriarchy (Cf Friend, 1912, Gurdon, 1907, Thurston, 1909, Briffault, 1927). Matriarchy implies the dominance of women in decision making. Authority is vested in her, both in theory and in practise. She is the channel not merely for inheritance, but also for succession to positions of authority in the family. Bachofen's theory that matriliny (descent through women) and matriarchy (rule by women) were but two aspects of the same institution is also disputable. From the perspective of cultural evolution, it is quite probable that the two aspects were combined. But, there are several instances where lineality is not necessarily associated with power. Schneider (1961:viii) writes, "...the generalised authority of women over men, as imagined by Bachofen, was never observed in known matrilineal societies, but only recorded in legends and myths. Thus the whole notion of matriarchy fell rapidly into disuse in anthropological work". Gabrielle Bertrand (1958) has written years back a popular book "Secret Lands where Women Reign" dealing partly with the Khasi and the Jaintia Hills. It was not factual and criticised by some as "a very false one, for the lands was by no means secret, and women do not reign there" (Shadap-Sen, 1981).

Spread of Matrilineal Communities in India

The people of India have a variety of kinship systems and they can be broadly categorised into three types; patrilineal, matrilineal, and bilineal. Barring two important pockets of people following matrilineal systems in the south-west and north-east part of India, rest of Indian population is predominantly patrilineal. People following bilateral systems, with both parents being relevant for reckoning kinship and for claiming rights to resources are comparatively few in Indian population. There are also communities which reckon descent matrilineally but follow patrilineal mode of inheritance and succession patterns. In India matriliny is highly diversified and transformed. The communities having matrilineal social systems exhibit no uniform matrilineal structure and differ from one community to another, and even among different subgroups of the same community. The present study focuses on the matrilineal system with special reference to the Khasi of Meghalaya.

Though matrilineal system was much more widely distributed in India, the matrilineal communities and the communities bearing matrilineal elements are chiefly found in the north-east and south-west parts of India (Raha 1989). The Khasis and Garos of Meghalaya are the important tribal groups who follow the matrilineal system in the north-east part of India.

Though neighbours geographically, the two communities are distinct with reference to the structure and composition of the descent groups and with relation to inheritance and residence patterns.

The Garos, a Scheduled Tribe of Meghalaya, follow matrilineal descent system. They are divided into a number of groups related to geographical area although they do not have much of cultural differences. The various Garo groups are Chisak, Matchi, Matabeng, Ambengdual or Matchi dual, Atong, Ganching, Chibak, Ruga, Megam, Koch or Kotchu. The Garos are internally divided into two exogamous matrilineal phratries (*chatchi* or *machong)* – Sangma and Marak which intermarry. At present there is a third group, Momin which is originated by historical process of marriage with non-Garo women (Nakane, 1961). Majumdar (1978) has reported the existence of two more new exogamous matrilineal groups' viz. Sira and Areng. The *chatchi* are further segmented into many localised lineages. (The native term *mahari* is also used to refer the localised lineages as well).

Among the Garos property is inherited in the female line. One of the daughters (not necessarily the youngest one) is selected by the parents to be the inheritress. If a couple has no female child than a girl belonging to the *machong* of the wife (preferably the daughter of her sister, real or classificatory) is adopted to be the inheritress. The girl selected to be the inheritress is known as *nokna dongipa mechik* (one who has been kept or meant for the household). The husband of the inheritress is known as *nokrom*. A *nokrom* should preferably be the real nephew of the father of the *nokna*. Residence after marriage is matrilocal. A son-in law who is not a *nokrom* is known as *agate* (one remaining outside) (Majumdar, 1978).

Rabhas, a tribal community of West Bengal, who traditionally followed matrilineal system, is now in a transitional stage from matriliny to patriliny. In West Bengal they are mostly found in Jalpaiguri and Cooch Behar districts. They are also found in neighbouring states of Assam and Meghalaya. The matrilineal system persisted significantly among a section of them who inhabited in the settlements inside the reserve forests while it was steadily declining among the village dwelling groups due to the influence of local Hindu society adopting the patrilineal mode of social system.

The Rabha community is divided in to a number of clans called *husuks* and the clan into sub-clans (*neoya husuk*). The clans are exogamous and a good number of them are totemic in nature. Though the forest Rabhas observe the rule of clan exogamy strictly, the village Rabhas, in recent years, have relaxed this rigidity a little and they are following the Hindus of the area. They are nowadays inclined to prohibit marriage in father's *husuks* which was not a practice earlier. The *husuks* among them have the twin functions of control of marriage and control of passing of property to a member of another *husuk*. The forest Rabhas still follow the community endogamy while the village Rabhas are not. The rules of inheritance and succession are different among two sections of the Rabhas. Among the forest Rabhas, the property (movable) is owned by the females and inherited by daughters, preferably the youngest one. The immovable property is assumed to be officially owned by the father (though actually they are owned by the forest department) and the same is inherited by the daughter's husband from the father. In the case of village Rabhas the property, both movable and immovable, is owned by the males and the rules of inheritance follow the male line. The forest Rabhas, after marriage follow duolocal residence initially and then change to uxorilocal or neolocal type of residence where as the village Rabhas follow the virilocal pattern of residence. In marriages the forest Rabhas prefers village endogamy whereas the other group prefer marriages from other villages (Raha, 1989).

Another community which shows matrilineal features in eastern and north-eastern parts of the country are the Lalung. The Lalung population is found scattered in the different parts of Assam with large concentration in Nowgong and Kamrup districts of Assam. They are also found in the some parts of Meghalaya as well. The Lalung call themselves Tiwas. Their society is divided into twelve clans *(kul)* which are again divided into a number of sub-clans. Rule of residence after marriage among them is generally matrilocal. Inheritance is sought through the female line and after the death of the mother her youngest daughter receives all her property. Though they still follow rules of matriliny, yet recently in some cases authority has shifted from the mother to the father and after his death his youngest son has been chosen as the next head. Instead of the youngest daughter or son, other daughters and sons are also getting some share of their parents' property these days (Sarit Chaudhuri, 1994).

The Nayar of Kerala was a classical example for matrilineal communities in India. The Thiyyar of North Kerala and Mappilas of north Kerala and Lakshadweep islands were also matrilineal at one point of time. Interestingly, a section of the Namboodiri Brahmins of North Kerala (Payyanur Brahmins) had followed the matrilineal system till a few decades back (the rest of Namboodiri Brahmins in Kerala have been the strict observants of patrilineal system). The males of this community are called Thirumumbus and the females Thampayis till their marriage and after that

Amma Thirumumbu. Many of the tribal communities in Kerala (like Kanikkar, Mala Ullada, etc.) followed the matrilineal system of descent and inheritance pattern and some others like Mullukuruma followed matrilineal descent but inheritance was patrilineal. The Arumbukuttom Vellalas of Tamil Nadu numbering a few thousands of people still follow the matrilineal system of descent and inheritance (M.Sasikumar, 1999). There is no reference of this community in the early literature. Even the Edgar Thurston's monumental volumes on "Castes and Tribes of Southern India" (1907) do not contain any information on them. The "People of India Volumes on Tamil Nadu (Vol-XL-1997) also does not give any trace of this community. The Arumbukuttam Vellalar is an endogamous group with no sub-divisions among them. But there exists a principal variety of descent group called *kilai*, which is equal to the English word lineage. It is a unilineal descent group. Members of a group reckon the descent in each generation from the epical ancestor. Each such *kilai* is an exogamous group and marriage between its members is prohibited. The right over the property (both movable and immovable) is rested on the women of the family. Property transmission is done from mother to daughters. In the absence of the latter, it will go to the former's sisters and their daughters. In the past, men surrender whatever possession he earned by his own to his sisters and their daughters and never to his own children. Some deviations can be observed to this rule today as a few of them have passed their earned property to their own children. If the spouses of his own children were nieces and nephews of his own (through the preferred system of cross cousin marriages), such transmission of property normally would not create any stress or strain in the community.

Their properties are of two types; ancestral and self-earned. Formerly when duo local residence was in vogue, the eldest male member of the family managed the ancestral property, but he had no right to alienate any portion of it and transmitted through the female line. The Arumbukuttam Vellalar followed the duo local form of residence in the past. The wives continue to stay in her natal home and her husband visiting her occasionally. Duo locality is often associated with matrilineal decent. Recently there occurred substantial changes in the residence rules from duo local to matrilocal, whereby the couple is expected to reside with the wife's relatives after marriage. This has caused for the structural changes in the composition of joint families. The joint family found among the Arumbukuttam Vellalar today is only a conglomeration of a few nuclear families.

The other Tamil castes and communities like Kottai Vellallar, Maravar and Illathu Pillamars also followed matrilineal descent but had not adopted matrilineal inheritance and succession patterns (Thurston, 1975). The Maravar community comprises different subgroups like Kondaiyamkottai, Ambaneri, Anjukottu and Karana Maravar and all these sub-castes still sustain the matrilineal descent system while the other matrilineal components could not co-exist. Presently, for all these sub-castes of Maravar the residence after marriage is patrilocal, male equigeniture is the rule of inheritance and succession is on the male line (Bharati: 2004).

The Kurichians, a tribal community of Kerala, is well known for their matrilineal system of kinship and descent. Among them the ancestral properties are owned collectively and inheritance is strictly matrilineal. The wives stay with their husbands and they rejoin her natal family when their husbands die or when they get divorced. This combination of partly patrilocal residence and matrilineal descent, though described as dysfunctional by some authors (Driver in Honigmann (ed.), 1975:338), had been a characteristic feature of the Nairs of North Kerala for centuries (c.f. Gough, 1961:390, 399) and which still continues among the Kurichias (M.Sasikumar 1996).

Review of literature

Studies on Khasis: There are a number of research studies on the Khasis by anthropologists and other social scientists. The first full-fledged study on the Khasi ethnography is "the Khasis" by Gurdon published in 1907. It gives a systematic account of the Khasi, their manners and customs, their ethnological affinities, their laws and institutions, religion, folklore, and their language. The book follows more or less the same pattern of description adopted by the British administrators turned anthropologists of their time. Till the publication of Gurdon's "The Khasis", information on Khasis were scattered in different administrative and census reports, Bulletins and journals. Before Gurdon, Mills (1853) prepared a report on the Khasi and Jaintia hills and U. Jeebon Roy published his Ka Niam Jong Ki Khasi (1897). In 1934 an important publication came out "Notes on Khasi Law" by Cantile.

The publication of "The History and culture of Khasi people" (1967) by Hamlet Barreh, which perhaps is the first attempt of its kind , that too by a Khasi Man, which presents the Khasi history based on all available sources of information. It contains a detailed treatment on many basic subjects of ethnography, culture, politics and history. Emphasis in this work was laid on the evolution of Khasi society, i.e. the matrilineal form of organization, its megalithic and religious aspects reviewed in light of their chronological history and the nature of their civil institutions. The chapter on "Society and Culture" is particularly relevant as it deals with the origin and evolution of Khasi society and development of their culture.

The Khasi Canvas by JN Choudhury (1978) would perhaps be the first venture after Gurdon's "The Khasis" to present in a single handy volume most of the important aspects of Khasi life. The author in this volume followed the conventional ethnographic style of description of material covering a wide range of subjects. A full chapter was devoted to discuss Khasi matriliny and followed a comparative approach in discussion.

Mathur followed a different approach in studying the Khasi society. His book "The Khasi of Meghalaya' (1979) is a study in tribalism and religion. The inter relationship between religious forces and political system with regard to the matrilineal systems operative among the Khasi was the subject matter of the study. The author had shown particular interest in investigating the Khasi's exposure to the outside world for the last 150 years or more and found that it had impinged on the traditional system and new patterns have emerged out of the adjustments between the extraneous elements and the traditional forms. The book has a full chapter on the Muslim Khasis in which the author endeavoured to examine the nature, extend and consequences of Khasi contact with the Muslim and the persistence of tribal traits in spite of their conversion and prolonged period of contact with the Muslims.

Emic studies on the Khasis were not few. Many Khasis have written about their own community from different perspectives and expositions. Mawrie's "The Khasi Milieu" (1981) is a study belonging to this category. In brief in seventeen chapters he exposed the nature of Khasi life in its true perception. He dealt with all aspects of nature, man and spirit complexes surrounding the Khasi society and also dealt with the social structure and life of the people. The emic experiences of the author have been explained with a literary talent. He writes "a father's status in the family is unique. The sound of his *hookah* brings security to the household and his coughing symbolises the strengths and power that control the household".

The book "Origin and Early History of Khasi- Synteng People" by Shadap-Sen (1981) makes a detailed study of the prehistory and earlier history of the Khasi people. In the first part it throws new light on the Ahom kingdom and in the second part attempts to present a picture of the life of the Khasis before they were exposed to western influence.

Dasgupta (1984) studied the War Khasis, one of the subdivisions of Khasis who live down the southern slopes of Meghalaya. The author followed the same pattern of description as in conventional ethnographic studies and it dealt with different aspects of life of War Khasi, like material culture, economic, social and political life and belief systems.

Chowdhury's book "The Khasi people" (1996) presents various facets of the Khasi matriliny in so far as it conforms to, and differs from, other extant matrilineal societies in light of recent anthropological findings. The megalithic heritage of the Khasis in the global perspective of archaeological and prehistoric movement of megalithic culture from the Stone Age was also dealt with in this volume. Though the author had drawn heavily from his earlier publication, "The Khasi Canvas" (1978), the book offers a lot of additional information on Khasis and analyses the Khasi matrilineal system in terms of tradition, continuity and change. He observes that the first challenge to Khasi matriliny came from under the impact of Christianity. The passage the Khasi matriliny had passed over years was no longer smooth, it had been called up on to adjust to the demands of time. The grumblings of discontent against the matrilineal system had been heard from time to time.

One of the writers who constantly made felt her presence through her journalistic but critical over view of the Khasi social setting is the journalist cum activist Patricia Mukhim. As an insider of the community she constantly tried to understand the Khasi social psyche. She wrote several papers on the Khasi way of life (1999, 2002a, 2002b, 2003 and 2004). Patricia Mukhim observes "Khasis might like to be reminded that they have changed their world view drastically with the advent of Christianity. They have given up much of their cultural persuasions, including their dances, songs, manner of dressing, eating, etc." (2002a). She makes a self-assessment of matriliny in the community. "We have convinced ourselves that matriliny is indeed a great cultural showcase. We therefore see only the utopian idea of matriliny instead of moving forward to bring structural changes in the system wherever necessary so that it can stand the test of time. Time not as in a stationary vehicle but as a dynamic, moving entity" (2002a). Mukhim (1999) in her paper "Crisis of authority in the Khasi matrilineal system" dealt with in some detail the influence of matriliny in the formulation of male personality and its divergent ramifications. It creates a feeling of inferiority and insecurity in the male from the beginning and sets in frustration and makes them grow irresponsible.

Later on many social scientists belonging to the community tried to understand the various manifestations of influence of matrilineal system in their society. Rynjah, (1999) in the paper "the Khasi family – dynamic role of father and maternal uncle" observed that aberrations arise within the matrilineal system mostly due to the change in value systems and the over-consciousness of its members on the materialistic side of the system. He observed that they have failed to analyse the spiritual side of such a family for which the custom had emerged up on. There is discontentment among the Khasi males, especially among the youth, which should be removed by enlightenment about the custom of olden days. Syiem (1999) wrote about the transitional phase of Khasi matriliny and felt that some kinds of stress and strain are evident in that society and witness a decreasing influence of the matrilineal group on its members because of many factors like spread of education, urbanization and many other factors. What is observable today in Khasi matriliny is a painful transition and change.

Is matriliny an impediment to entrepreneurship in Khasi society? Passah (1999) finds that the socio-cultural system being followed by Khasis and other communities of the state like Jaintias and Garos does not support or contribute to the emergence of local entrepreneurship in many aspects of their socio-economic life. He observed that the British recognition of the rights of the youngest daughters as legal heiress to all family properties to the exclusion of sons and other daughters in the family, makes the sons or nephews ineligible to succeed to his business concerns although they have developed skill and capability to run and sustain it, and the son-in-law who runs the business, as coming from another familial environment may not have the skill and subsequently collapse the business.

Today a number of Khasi scholars themselves have begun to critically scrutinise the social system of the community at different levels and at different perspectives. Many articles on academic and popular journals are currently available. It is neither possible nor feasible to review all of them. Some such studies have been quoted or referred in the discussion part of this book wherever necessary to substantiate the findings of this study.

Studies on Matriliny: Studies on the matrilineal system are not recent in anthropological literature. Nineteenth and twentieth century anthropologists studied matrilineal systems from the evolutionary and functional point of view. Richard's (1950) comparative study of Central Bantu matrilineal societies marked a major advance in the analysis of matrilineal descent groups. The publication of "Matrilineal Kinship" (ed. by Schneider and Gough in 1961) is a remarkable achievement in the series of studies in this field. It offers analytical accounts of a wide variety of matrilineal societies spreading from North America to Africa and to India.

Aiyappan's (1990) study of Kurichian matrilineal system is another outstanding contribution to this field. Though the Kurichians still follow the matrilineal system of kinship and descent many of the associated institutions began to dwindle due to the functioning of extraneous elements. The land reforms enforcing ceiling on land holdings implemented by the Kerala State Government caused for the disintegration of the matrilineal joint families of the Kurichians. The Japanese Anthropologist Chi Nakane's (1967) comparative study of Garo and Khasi matrilineal systems is another well-known effort in this line. The study focuses on the differences in the structures of matrilineal systems with reference to each other and in relation to other matrilineal systems. The study is mainly a comparative theoretical treatise on the Garo and Khasi matrilineal systems. She theorised that the unilineal principle (matrilineal system) works differently in each given society producing different structures and descent principle and residence are equally important criteria for the analysis of social organization.

Another major work in this area of study is Raha's (1989) book on Rabhas, which concentrates on a paradigm shift that is taking place among them from matrilineal system to the patrilineal. The study reveals that the two ecological sections of the Rabhas- the forest Rabhas and the village Rabhas- though consider themselves as belonging to the same group, had undergone different types of cultural influences. The forest Rabhas continue to be more or less isolated thanks to the prevailing forest rules which prohibit the entry of the outsiders to their settlements and thus could maintain the cultural homogeneity of the group, whereas the same degree of cultural homogeneity was not found among the village Rabhas where various groups of people belonging to Hindu, Muslims, and tribes are inhabiting adjacent to them. They are interdependent up on each other and their present day culture reflects a clear picture borrowing of the non-Rabhas cultural elements. The rapid development of the cash and the market economy and also the implementation of the new administration, new legislation including new land reform acts, new educational systems, development in transport and communication systems, etc., help to bring varied degrees of changes in their culture. At the same time the semi isolated condition of the habitat could help the forest dwelling Rabhas to preserve their traditional matrilineal culture to a considerable extent.

Govindanunny's (1994) book "Kinship Systems in South and South East Asia-A Study" is a study on matrilineal system of Minangkabaus of West Sumatra, in Indonesia and he made an effort to compare the Minangkabau system with that of Nair system of Kerala. The study established that the main principle of matrilineal culture in both the communities is broadly the same: matrilineal descent, matrilineal clans, clan exogamy, clan authority theoretically in the hands of the mother, but rarely exercised by her in practise, authority of the mother's brother and succession of authority from mother's brother to sister's daughter. But the major difference is perhaps only in one aspect; among the Minangkabau the rule of lineage descent from the same ancestress and inheritance of ancestral property is limited to five generations. The fifth generation will be considered a separate lineage unit or assuming clan with a separate ancestress. The rule is significant in that marriage exogamy will not be present and to men of new group girls of the parent unit, whom they were formerly unable to marry, now became legitimate potential wives. The fifth generation split is unique among the Minangkabau.

Systematic studies are yet to be undertaken to understand the current problems peculiar to each such societies in the backdrop of matrilineal systems prevalent among them. The present study discusses the social systems of the Khasis in detail from both historical and present perspectives. It also tries to understand the structure of the role, power and function of both men and women in a social system where the position of women has been said to be more comfortable due to the matrilineal system.

The reasons for choosing to attempt a comparison of Khasi matrilineal system with that of Nair system were initially out of curiosity. The first exposure to the researcher to the Khasi society made him feel the steadfastness of the community in keeping the elements of matrilineal system as strictly as possible even though other aspects of their culture including the religion and belief systems had undergone drastic changes. The researcher was familiar with the factors which brought drastic changes in the Nair matrilineal system such as the impact of cash economy, western style education, improved communication facilities, British imposed and interpreted law on the complex social structure, etc. The eagerness was to understand how far these factors are present in the Khasi society and how it is operating and if it is evident in that society how the structural mechanism is resisting the changes. But the comparison did not limit only to Nairs and wherever the comparable data are available, but has attempted to compare it with other matrilineal societies, like Kurichians of Kerala, Arumbukuttam Vellalas of Tamilnadu, Rabhas, Garos, etc.

Area of the study

Fieldwork for the present study was conducted in the Nongkrem and Sawmer villages of East Khasi Hills District of Meghalaya for six weeks each. Nongkrem is located in the eastern most corner of the East Khasi Hills district about ten Kilometres away from the Shillong city, the capital of the State. The plateau of the Khasi hills ranges from about 5000 feet to 6000 feet high. The Shillong peak, which is about 6445 feet high, situates very near to the Nongkrem village. The etymological meaning of the word Nongkrem is 'village of caves'. *Nong* in Khasi means village and *krem* means caves, and thus Nongkrem means the village of caves. Several natural caves are found in this village. According to a folk story prevalent among the Khasis, the origin of the Syiems of Smit and Mylliem is associated with one of these caves. The story tells like this: a young beautiful girl was living in one of the caves called *Marai*. Being attracted by her beauty many people tried to approach her but only to be disappointed as she immediately withdrew in to the narrow recess of the cave. But a clever and brave man of Mylliam-Ngap clan decided to trap her by any means. One day he had shown her a bunch of beautiful flowers and thus attracted her out of the cave. Then the man could catch hold of her and she was brought to the village. The parents of the young man offered his hand in marriage to this girl and their progenies are believed to be the present day Syiems. She is considered as the primordial mother and the first high priestess (*Syiem Sad*) of the Khyrim Syiemship. Her name was Pah Syntiew derived from two root words *pah* meaning 'lure someone' and *syntiew* meaning flower thus *pah syntiew* meaning 'someone who is lured by a flower'.

The entire village of Nongkrem is divided into eleven localities. They are: (i) Warbah (ii) Rngikseh (iii) Kharbuli (iv) Nongryndong (v) Mawlynnei (vi) Mawpynthaw (vii) Iewpumtiah (viii) Kyntunumon (ix) Mawmuthuh (x) Urmasiujoh and (xi) Lamlyer. Each village has a Council known as Durbar or *Durbar Shnong* and an elected village headman (*Rangbah Shnong*) heads each locality and all the adult male members were its members. All these localities together constitute a village council called *Raid* for the purpose of social control and harmonious civil and judicial administration. At the *Raid* level it consists of one Lynskor, one Lyngdoh and four Myntris. The Myntris always act as councillor to the headman as well as to the Syiem's council. The Lynskor is from Mylliem-Ngap clan, the Lyngdoh from the Lyngdoh clan and one each of the Myntries from Pyngrup, Mylliam Pdah, Warbah and Khyriem Mujat clans respectively.

Data for the present study was collected from the entire village spread in all the eleven localities but the household survey was confined to the Rngikseh and Kharbuli localities. It was told that the original seat of the Khyrim Syiemship was in Nongkrem and later on it was shifted to the nearby Smit area. The Nongkrem dance (*Shad Nongkrem*), the annual dance festival of Khasis performed at Smit at the house premises of the *Syiem Sad* (high priestess) is known after the name of this village.

The Sawmer village, the second village selected for the study, is located about five kilometres away from Shillong town on the southwest direction. As the name Sawmer indicates ('Saw' means four and 'mer' means miles in Khasi language), the village situates on the fourth mile from Shillong town on the Shillong Cherrapunjee road. The village comprises four localities namely Pdengshnong, Three and Half Mile, Pynthor, and Four and half Mile. 'Pdeng' means centre and 'shnong' means village and thus Pdengshnong means central village/locality. 'Pynthor' means adjacent meaning that it is an adjacent village or locality to the Pdengshnong.

The village is in a semi-urban setting with a majority of people working in central/state government services. A sizeable section of the people is also found engaged in petty businesses as well. The number of people working in agricultural-oriented sector is comparatively few. The earliest settlers of this village were the members of the Kharkonger clan. Now people from different clans like Shabong, Tron, Jyrwa, Nongbet, Kharmnuid, Syiemlieh, Wajri, Paswet, Syiem, Lyngwa, Thankiew, Nongtraw, Majaw, Lyngdoh, Deingdoh, Kharshiing, Hynniewta, Nongkynrih, Kharmaphlang, Nongrum, Synrem, etc., are found settled in this village. All the four localities together have a headman (*Rangbah Shnong)*. Each locality has an assistant headman (assistant Rangbah Shnong) who works under the direction of the headman. One of the assistant headmen is to be from Kharkonger clan, a privilege being accorded to the early settlers of the village. There is also an elected executive committee known as *Rengbah Dong*. The Electoral College to elect these office bearers includes all the adults of the village, both male and female. Contrary to the tradition women in this village were permitted to take part in the activities of the village durbar but their involvement in its functioning was very much limited.

*****

Chapter - II

The Khasi People

The home land of Khasi people is the state of Meghalaya. "Meghalaya" is a Sanskrit term meaning 'the abode of clouds'. It was christened so by the geographer Suniti Kumar Chatterjee, who noticed excessive clouds here, making it one of the rainiest areas in the world. From 1926 to 1932 he visited the place frequently and produced a doctoral thesis titled 'Geographical Analysis of Meghalaya', which was submitted to Paris University. The name Meghalaya received unanimous acceptance when the Home Ministry, Government of India, was looking for a suitable name for the newly created state consisting of the Khasi, Jaintia and Garo Hills.

Meghalaya emerged as an autonomous state on 2nd April 1970 and as a full-fledged state on January 1972, marking the beginning of a new era in the geo-political history of North-East India. The state shares its border with Assam on the north and the Bangladesh on the south. It covers an area of 22,429 sq. kilometers and extends for about 300 kilometers from west to east and 100 kilometers from north to south. According to 2011 Census, it has a total population of 2,966,889 with 1,491,832 males and 1,475,057 females. The overall density of population in the state is 132 persons per sq. kilometers which is lower than national average of 382 per square kilometers.

Meghalaya is the homeland of many tribal communities predominant among them being Khasis, Garos, and Jaintias. Constellations of other tribal communities like Lalung, Hajong, Man, Dalu, Boro, Mikir, Rabha, and Koch and a host of linguistic and religious groups like Bengali, Nepali, Assamese, Bihari, Marwari, Muslim, and Sikh, were also found inhabiting the state. The state invited the attention of anthropologists, social scientists and the non-academicians alike for decades as the abode of three major communities practising matriliny. But the three communities have distinct identities with reference to their social customs and practises, art, craft, and architecture, religious beliefs and practises, political institutions, language and dialect, etc., were concerned and occupy specific geographic areas and the common factor being the matrilineal system of descent.

The Khasis, more than half-a-million in strength, is one of the most advanced tribal communities in India. They are well known in literature as a community practicing matrilineal system of descent and inheritance and even, though wrongly, often quoted as an example of 'matriarchal' societies in India. They speak a dialect that belongs to Mon-Khmer branch of the Austric family forming a linguistic island amidst of Tibeto-Burman speaking communities of north-east India. The origin of the term Khasi is ascribed to two root words 'kha' and 'si'. *Kha* in Khasi means 'born of' and *si* refers to an 'ancient mother'. So they together means 'born of ancient mother'.

Myth of Origin

Every community would have its own stories and folk tales regarding its origin. The Khasis also have their own tales about the origin of the community. The Khasi tradition is that they are the progenies of the people of the original seven huts (*Hynniew Trep)* out of the sixteen huts created by God. All of them lived in the Heaven along with God. Sins were unknown to them at that point of time. God decreed that the Hynniew Trep should populate the world and hence they came down to the earth. But still they maintained their relationship with the rest of the members of nine huts *(Khyndai Trep*) and God. A ladder (also said to be a golden bridge) connected the earth with the Heaven (the Golden bridge was believed to be situated in Lumsohpet Bneng near Umroi). Later on, one of the members of the Hynniew Trep pulled down the ladder in order to stop the dominance of God over them. God retorted by plunging the world in darkness. The members of the Hynniew Trep prayed to God and a cock came to the rescue of the Hynniew Trep and he mediated between God and the Hynniew Trep. He went to the sun and took upon himself all the blame for the sinful act. The sun was pleased and dispelled the darkness that enveloped the earth and thus re-established the relationship between God and the men at earth but not in the same way, as it was earlier. The cock since then became sacred and the most important sacrificial bird (Mathur, 1979:62).

Many writers (like Gurdon, Hutton, Chatterji and Lyngdoh) entertained the idea that the Khasis have migrated from the eastern direction and settled in their present habitat. These are all inferences based on the historical facts and archaeological remains and linguistic and cultural traits. Bareh (1985) stated the possibility that the ancient Khasis were immigrants somewhere from the Cambodia region and from the banks of the Mekong River.

Divisions among the Khasis

Four subdivisions of Khasis are generally identified. They are the Jaintias, the War Khasis, the Lyngam Khasis and the Khasi proper or the mainland Khasis or the Khynriam Khasis. These subdivisions of Khasis are not strict endogamous groups, but they are not exogamous as well. Among these subgroups there were many similarities as well as differences. The differences are observable mainly in dialects and in some of the cultural practises and observances of religious rites and rituals. They were not strict endogamous groups because inter-marriages among them were not strictly prohibited and there were no stigmas attached with if such marriages were to happen and the children of such marriages were considered as the full-fledged members of the mother's group. It is not strictly exogamous as well, because intermarriages among them were not of very common occurrence.

Marriages between them, though uncommon, were not prohibited. The Lyngams were said to be half-Khasi and half-Garo (Gourdon 1975:62). Some of the authors like Gourdon (1975) and Chowdhury (1996) considered the Bhois also as a subgroup of Khasis though there was certain admixture of Mikir elements in them. The Bhois themselves claim that they are Khasis and many Khasi customs and social traits were reported to be present side by side with Mikir influences in their culture. Though all the subgroups of Khasis share many things in common, differences were observed as far as many of their cultural elements such as economy, dialects, customs and rituals, etc., were concerned. All these sub-groups follow the matrilineal system of descent and kinship though there were differences in minutiae.

The present study was carried out among the Khasi proper (Khynriam Khasis) who inhabit the central high plateau. The Khynriam people were under two dynasties namely Khyrim and Mylliem, which are still extant. The divine origin of these two Syiemships was discussed earlier in connection with the story of Pah Syntiew. Tradition tells that both Khyrim and Mylliem branches, in the beginning, formed one integrated Syiemship for all purposes and was known as 'Ka Hima Shillong' (Chowdhury 1996:113). It was due to the active intervention in the succession dispute by the British since its occupation of the Khasi and Jaintia Hills in 1835, that the kingdom was finally divided into two independent Syiemships in 1858 (Mathur 1979:65). Though the advent of the British rule and the promulgation of Constitution of India since independence has taken away much of the Syiem's powers, the Syiems still plays a vital role in the administrative affairs of the tribe. Even now he takes decision in matters of tribal policies.

Origin of Matrilineal System

There were many theories of the origin of matrilineal system in the anthropological literature as discussed in the introductory chapter. But each community practicing matriliny has its own story of origin of such systems in their community, sometimes purely of fictional and sometimes based on historical facts and evidences. The historical background of the origin of the matrilineal system among the Khasis was not known. Tradition says that during the historical periods the Khasis engaged in constant fights with their neighboring kingdoms and hence men folk were always away from home and family for long time and even their return was uncertain. Under such circumstances the women had to come forward to take over the responsibility of looking after the family (Mukhim, 1999). Since the return of the husbands from the war front was uncertain the women might also enter in to remarriages every now and then. Such a situation compelled them to adopt a system of descent and inheritance convenient to the situation. The descent through the maternal line makes the fathers identity unimportant as far as the descent of the children is concerned and this system helped them to identify themselves with their mothers' group even when the identity of their fathers was not indefinite. This was said to be the historical context in which the matrilineal system originated and developed among the Khasis.

More or less similar explanations of origin of matrilineal systems were available among the Nairs of Kerala as well. The Nairs were a warrior class under different local chieftains who ruled the different Nadu-s (Chiefdoms). Constant fights between neighboring Chiefdoms for territorial expansion of Chiefdoms was a regular occurrence and the Nairs constituted the militia of each such Chiefdom. The explanation was that the matrilineal system developed to cope with such a situation of men always keeping away from home to ensure the social security of the women and children. The Nair profession as warriors began to dwindle after the British administration in India began to overlook the Nair cavalry as a reliable force to meet their needs and the setting up of permanent armies with modern arms and ammunitions.

Economy

The backbone of Khasi economy is agriculture and petty trade. The main crop cultivated by the Khasis is the potato. Mr. David Scott, the Governor General's agent on the frontier, dates back in 1830, introduced potato cultivation among them. Still then this is the major crop of the Khasis. Long back, before the potato cultivation became so extensive, they cultivated rice and some millets and the cultivation was of shifting cultivation type. This practice was abolished since the forest wealth of this area become denuded. Even now the relics of this mode of cultivation can be observed in their present day potato cultivation practices. They cultivate potato at a plot continuously for a period of three to four years and then allow the land to be fallow for a few years until the area rejuvenated with vegetation. This will help to regain the lost fertility of the soil.

Besides potatoes, green peas and cabbages, different varieties of bananas are also raised by the villagers. Oranges, pineapples, ginger, etc., are also being cultivated by the Khasis but in a small scale. Orchard is greatly in vogue in the Khasi Hills. Areca-nut gardens are a common scene in War-Khasi areas. Pineapple gardens in Nongpoh areas are expanding very fast. These products are sold through the weekly markets or they would bring them to the Shillong town where they found ready customers for these products especially among the government servants settled in and around the Shillong city. Buses loaded with baskets of vegetables coming down to the Shillong city are a common scene. The market at Bara Bazar is the major one. There are also markets at Laitumukhra, Polo etc. Traditionally they sold out their products through the weekly markets. The weekly markets are still functioning though some like the one at Nongkrem are not so active. Based on the weekly markets the Khasis have developed an eight day week calendar as well.

The market-oriented production of agricultural produces has introduced the Khasis to an acute commercial economy, which has brought about various changes in their social life. Earlier production was mainly subsistence based and transactions were of barter type. The production of agricultural products for the market introduced them to a commercial economy where in transactions is totally in terms of cash. This has also brought substantial changes in terms of production relations and the gaps between the rich and poor widened resulting in emergence of different economic classes. Land which was plenty earlier and was controlled by the clan (*ri-kur*) and the community (*ri-raid*) was distributed among the needy members for cultivation. Once the land became scarce it increasingly began to be considered as an economic asset capable of buying and selling and the female ultimogeniture rule of inheritance helped to concentrate the landed property in the hands of youngest daughters neglecting other children. Now one can observe different classes of people in the Khasi society based on economic conditions; an upper class majority of them are city dwellers, a middle class who are mainly the government servants working in different state and central government offices and other institutions combined with some other earnings from business and a working class predominantly from villages.

The land among the Khasis was owned by the family and was managed by the maternal uncle of the youngest daughter who later inherited the property. But nowadays some differences are observed to this pattern and in many cases the husbands of the *ka khadduh* (youngest daughter) are found managing the family property of their wives for their sake.

Two patterns of land ownership were found in the studied villages:1). the land owned by the clan or *kur* called *ri-kur;* and 2). The land owned by the individual families known as *ri kynti*. The clan land cannot be alienated or transacted without the consent of the *kur* durbars. This property was looked after by the *kni* (the eldest of the maternal uncles) of the main family. In the case of the second type of property the family concerned was free to use the land as per its wish. Besides this there is a sacred grove (*law kyntang*) on the margin of many of the villages belonging to the whole village and they generally venerate this grove and do not cut trees from it except for the funeral of the village authorities like Syiem and Lyngdoh. There were also *ri-raid* lands which remain with the whole community. Each individual with in the area has got a right to cultivate and this right is confined to use and occupation only and such occupants cannot transfer or sublet it. If the occupant left it fallow for more than three years it would go back to the community and can be given to any other person for cultivation. If the occupant had made some permanent improvements on the land like construction of houses or raising permanent crops, etc., he may acquire permanent, heritable and transferable right over such land (LRI, 1984:55).

Those who do not own any landed property to cultivate, usually hired it for rent from fellow villagers for cultivation. Such hiring of land is in terms of *nur,* a measure of land approximately equal to fifteen feet length and three feet width. One *nur* is rented for an amount of five rupees per annum for a period of three years. The rent has to be paid in advance. Usually the entire family will go to the field and engage themself in different types of work. One may stay back to do the household chores. Children after their school hours also join their parents in both household and agricultural works whenever required.

Table 1: Land Holdings among the Khasis (Nongkrem)

Amount of Land	*No of Families*
Up to 1 Acre	16
Up to 2 Acres	14
Up to 3 Acres	20
More than 3 Acres	0
Total	**50**

Source: Fieldwork

Out of the total fifty families surveyed in the Nongkrem village sixteen families hold just one or below one acre of land and fourteen families possess one to two acres of land. The remaining twenty families hold up to three acres of land. Not a single family had more than three acres of land under their possession. It shows that the villagers were facing scarcity of land and hence those who depend on agriculture had to hire land for cultivation from fellow villagers.

Table 2: Land Holdings among the Khasis (Sawmer)

Amount of Land	*No of Families*
No land	17
Up to 1 Acre	63
Up to 2 Acres	6
Up to 3 Acres	5
More than 3 Acres	9
Total	**100**

Source: Fieldwork

The land holding pattern in Sawmer village gives a slightly different picture compared to Nongkrem. Out of the hundred families surveyed in Sawmer, seventeen families did not have any land under their possession and are living in rented houses. Sixty-three families hold less than one acre of land and in many cases they owned just the house site. Only nine families held more than three acres of land among them. This differential pattern was because of the particular geographical location of the village. As it is a semi-urban area many of the government employees and owners of small business establishments purchased their house sites and built houses there. Those who could not buy land are living in rented houses. Those families which owned more than one or two acres of land in Sawmer inherited it from ancestors.

Piggery is common among the Khasis. Most of the households have their own pigs and pig sheds. They relishes pork and it is one of the most common items of food. Pigs are reared for flesh both for domestic use as well as for sale. Cattle rearing were a rare activity and only one Khasi was found engaged in cattle rearing on a commercial basis. It is the locally settled Bihari people who meet the milk needs of the villagers. The Khasis prefer *lal chai* (red tea) to milk tea and the intake of milk and milk products were comparatively low.

A number of Khasis (both male and female) had got enrolled in the Central and State Government services. The Khasis were also found engaged in various other types of vocations, like petty trades, tea shops, vegetable and fruit stalls, grocery shops, fish stalls. In these activities the Khasi women dominated. There were some among them who were masters in iron fabrication, stone masonry, carpentry, etc. Many among them were government contractors as well. Some of them (especially women) were engaged in distilling country liquor or making rice beer for sale as well as for self-consumption. There was also a high demand for Khasi domestic help especially among the working middle class people settled in and around the Shillong town.

Table 3: Occupational Structure (Nongkrem)

Occupation	*Male*	*Female*	*Total*
Government Service	18	13	31
Petty Business	8	11	19
Daily Wage Labour	15	12	27
Agriculture	12	3	15
Contractors	8	0	8
Total	**61**	**39**	**100**

Source: Fieldwork

Out of the total working force 61% were males and 39% females in Nongkrem. Males dominate in all areas of work except in the field of petty trades. All contractors were men.

Table 4: Occupational Structure (Sawmer)

Occupation	*Male*	*Female*	*Total*
Government Service	50	20	70
Petty Business	12	12	24
Daily Wage Labour	16	5	21
Agriculture	12	2	14
Teachers	2	13	15
Others*	21	10	31
Total	**113**	**62**	**175**

Source: Fieldwork

*It includes Doctor (1), Veterinary Doctors (2), Air Hostess (1), Nurses (3), Tailors (3), Drivers (4), Carpenters (5), and Others (12).

The major source of income of the people in Sawmer was salary received by government servants. Out of the total working force 49% were in government service. Males outnumber females in all areas of work except in teaching, which is dominated by women. In business also women were at par with the men. Compared to Nongkrem, the number of daily wage earners is low. Those who inherited enough ancestral property adopted agriculture as profession. Out of the total working force 65% were males and 35% females.

Education

Education is one of the major indicatives of social development. It is also a prerequisite for socio-economic development and overall growth and advancement of any community. Even before independence, efforts to spread literacy among the Khasis were undertaken by missionaries. The Christian missions were active in spreading education among Khasis and they started a number of educational institutions to spread both primary and higher education among them. During the first half of the twentieth century, a number of educational institutions were opened and Shillong, the capital of erstwhile undivided Assam, became the centre of higher education in the whole of north-east India. Conversion to Christianity implied access to school education but it was not restrained to Christians alone.

The rate of male and female literacy among the Khasis does no have much difference but the drop outs at the primary and high school level was high among boys. The survey results in the two villages showed that girls were excelling boys especially in higher education.

The table below shows that the number of illiterates was more among females than males. But the number of people who attained higher education was high among females. It was evident that most of the boys discontinued their education after primary level. The girls outnumbered the boys as far as attaining high school, +2 education and graduation were concerned.

Table 5: Educational Status (Nongkrem)

Education	*Male*	*Female*	*Total*
Illiterates	15	25	40
Primary Education	55	40	95
High School Education	20	30	50
Matriculation	13	18	31
+2	13	13	26
Graduation	10	15	25
Total	**126**	**141**	**267**

Source: Fieldwork

Table 6: Educational Status (Sawmer)

Education	*Male*	*Female*	*Total*
Illiterates	54	59	113
Primary Education	79	87	166
High School Education	56	59	115
Matriculation	23	28	51
+2	31	48	79
Graduation	32	41	73
Post Graduation	0	5	5
BEd	0	5	5
Other*	5	6	11
Total	**280**	**338**	**618**

Source: Fieldwork

*It includes Law (1), BVSc (2), Bpharm (1), MBBS (1), Nursing (3), and Poly Technique (3).

In Sawmer at all levels of education the females dominated over males. The rate of dropouts was high among male students compared to female. The teachers of the nearby schools attested this very fact.

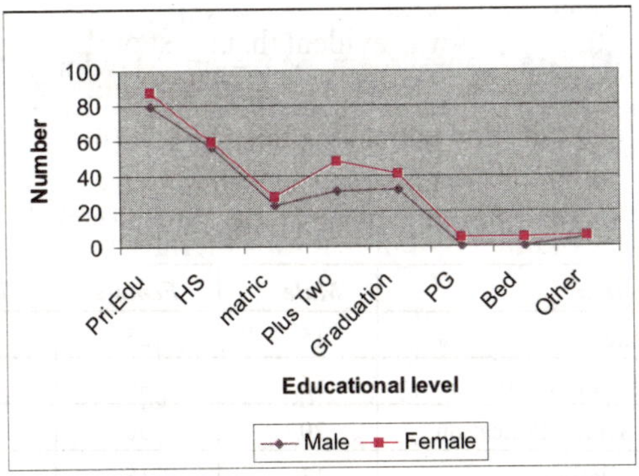

Source: Fieldwork.

Diagram I: Comparison of Level of Male and Female Education in Sawmer.

Traditional Political Organization

In the Khasi Hills, the traditional village councils (*Durbar Shnong*) with *Rangbah Shnong* as its head form the grass root level organization close to the people. The State (*Hima)* administration headed by the *Syiem* is at the highest level in a multi-tier system. Now it is under the administrative control of the constitutional District Council. In between *Durbar Shnong* and *Durbar Hima* there is an intermediate council called *Durbar Raid* presided by an official called *Sordar*. *Sordars* represents the commoners and were elected to office on the principle of the adult's (male) franchise. It is a political unit comprising a number of adjacent Khasi villages organized in a political system for the purpose of social control and harmonious civil and judicial administration. The power and functions of the traditional socio-political institutions have been greatly curtailed and marginalized by the Autonomous District Council (ADC), the key institution of the Sixth Schedule. With the introduction of District Councils, the traditional arrangement of local self-government became complex with overlapping jurisdiction. The ADC has powers over a large number of subjects pertaining to land and forest, customs and traditions, village and town administration including police, public health and sanitation. Besides the above powers the ADC can establish its own courts and make laws. It can also regulate the appointment and succession of chiefs and headmen. The laws passed by the Council have to be approved by the Governor (Gassah, 1997).

At present The Khasi Hills division has sixteen Syiemships-Khyrim, Mylliem, Nongkhlaw, Cherra, Rambrai, Myriaw, Nongstoin, Nobosohphoh, Mawiang, Nongspung, Maysynram, Maharam, Malai-sohmat, Langrin,

Bhowal and Jirang, three Lyngdohships-Mawphlang, Sohiong and Lyniong, five Sirdarships-Dwara Nongtyrnem, Mawdon, Mawlong, Nonglwai and Pamsanngut, and one Wahdadarship-Shella and all of them are now under the Autonomous District Council (H.Bareh, 1985:11). Certain Syiems have a divine origin called Syiem Blei (literally Syiems of God) while most of the other Syiems are called Syiem-briew or literally man Syiem (H.Bareh, 1985:35).

Lyngdohships and Basanships are non-Syiemship organizations evolved out of different historical process. Residents at a particular territory formed a village and entrusted a priest's family or kin (Lyngdoh) to conduct the affairs, both administrative and sacerdotal. They thus became the actual administrative and religious heads aided by a council of *Basans* in executive functions. The Basanships had a different route of evolution. Each colonizing clan occupied a strip of land and as its first occupant, it became a proprietor, entitled as such with permanent ownership of the land. Through further allegiances it extended its domain and its male leader, Rangbah kur or Basan became a ruler. Later on, various Lyngdohs and Basans combined and formed a Syiemship ordaining a princely dynasty to rule over a consolidated region (H.Bareh, 1985:39-40).

The village councils (*Durbar Shnong*) were not a fully representative body as the women were not its members and thus have no role in its functioning. Very recently, some durbars like one at Sawmer have started to include women of the respective area in the Electoral College to elect the headman but their involvement in the totality of its functioning was poor and partial. Another most commonly made critique against the traditional institution was the reservation of executive functions within the durbar to persons from certain particular clans. In Sawmer, the Kharkonger clan, being the earlier settlers of the village, has certain privileges. One of the assistants, *Rangbah Shnong,* should be from that clan.

One basic problem with the village level councils (*Durbar Shnong)* was that it was not supported by the necessary financial aids for its functioning as well as to plan and undertake development projects. Another drawback of the institution was that most of these durbars did not keep proper records of accounts of money they handle as traditionally, keeping records was not a custom and accounts by word of mouth was sufficient. Another difficulty in implementing the programmes at the village level was that the local level administrative bodies in Meghalaya were not constitutionally created but were traditional organizations. The Panchayati

Raj institutions which came into existence in the country with the 73rd Amendment to the Constitution has not yet been extended to the state of Meghalaya since the required resolutions have not yet been passed by the State Assembly. The Government of India constituted a committee of the Members of Parliament and experts on 10th June 1994 to suggest steps for harmonization of the Panchayati Raj institutions with the tribal areas and to formalize the salient features of a law to be enacted so that the provisions of the constitutional amendments may be extended to the tribal areas under article 243. Sri Dileep Singh Bhuria, MP was the Chairman. Only those areas comprised in the Fifth and Sixth Schedules of the constitution were under its purview.

The Bhuria committee emphasized that the traditional tribal conventions and laws should continue to be validly observed by them and that "modern systems" should be modulated so that there would be harmony with the traditional systems. The committee reiterated that most tribal societies have been practicing democracy in an egalitarian spirit and had already a series of indigenous institutions achieving a vital degree of decentralization. The participative character of these institutions was more advanced than the representative mechanisms adopted in modern systems.

In a path breaking enactment on 24th December 1996, the Parliament adopted a law (Central Act 40/1996) embodying virtually all the recommendations of the Bhuria committee. For the first time the concept of a "community" has been recognized in delineating the basic unit of local democracy. The "community" has been identified by culture and habitations; such community may be as small as it may occur in any given location ('hamlet' or 'small village'). If there are more than one such community in a village identified as such in any other context, then there shall be as many community wise panchayats as necessary, each autonomous within its specified identified territory. The Panchayati Raj Extension to Scheduled Areas Act 1996 (PESA) are hoped to give new life and direction to the decentralised planning drive in the state.

In recent years especially after the United Nation's declaration of the Year 1993 as the World Indigenous People's Year, there is a growing realization among the Khasi elites for a revival of their traditional Institutions and consequently campaigning for constitutional recognition for the traditional governing bodies began at various quarters. The poor performance of modern democratic institutions of governance in delivering proper administration made them think in this direction. The culmination of these campaigning was the grand assembly (or the ***People's Durbar)*** at Smit, a place of great politico-religious significance to Khasis on 14th January 2004. About 30,000 people participated in it. The explicit purpose of the assembly was to get people's approval for a massive development project.

Religion

The indigenous Khasi religion was based on the belief of God as the creator (*U Blei Nong-thaw*) with due respect for the ancestors. "The religion of the Khasis may be described as animism or spirit worship, or rather, the propitiation of spirits both good and evil on certain occasions principally in times of trouble" (Gourdon: 1907). As far as the Khasis were concerned, the religion and worship was a matrilineal family affair performed by the matrilineal male usually the *kni* (the eldest of the maternal uncles) at the *khadduh*'s residence. They have a community priest called *lyngdoh* but his services were not normally sought for family/lineage level worships and religious performances.

The Khasis never symbolise their gods by means of images, their worship being offered to the spirits only. Some such spirits worshiped by them are *Ulei muluk, Ulei umtong, Ulei longapah,* etc. (Gourdon, 1907: 106). The Khasis adore the deceased ancestors by means of periodical offerings. The cock is an important and sacred bird for the Khasis and it is sacrificed as part of their worship. Those who follow their traditional religion are specified as: "Khasi Khasis" and the Christian converts as Christian Khasis in this study for the sake of analysis.

Christianity

The first Christian Mission that could make some impact on the Khasis was the Welsh mission of the Presbyterian denomination. It sent its first missionary under the leadership of the Rev. Thomas Jones and his wife to Cherrapunjee, the then capital of the province, in 1841. It made a humble beginning but its impact on the culture of the hill people has been of far reaching consequence. Though initially the Christian missionaries faced stiff resistance from the Khasis, they later succeeded in converting them in to the Christian faith to a great extent. It was the Ka Nabon, the first Khasi woman, who was baptised in 1848 (Mathur 1979:16). The Roman Catholics started their missionary activities among the Khasis much later in 1890 and the strong spirit of competition among the various denominations helped in intensifying their activities. The Welsh Mission of the Presbyterian denomination when concentrated on primary education their Roman Catholic counterpart controlled the institutions for higher studies. They opened a number of reputed schools in Shillong like Loreto (1909) St.Mary's (1913), St.Edmund (1905), Don Bosco Training school (1923), and colleges like St. Antony's (1935), St Mary's (1935) and St. Edmund's (1937), and thus Shillong became the centre of higher education in the whole of north-east India (Mathur 1979:20). Though Christianity has now influenced a fairly large number of Khasis the structural aspects of the Khasi society have remained more or less intact.

The Seng Khasi Movement

The modern Seng Khasi (Seng in Khasi means an association or group) movement has been started as an attempt to safeguard the essence of Khasi culture, religion and custom from the onslaught of western and Christian influences. The Seng Khasi was established on 23rd November 1899 and ever since its establishment the 23rd November of every year is celebrated as the S*eng Kut Snem*. The Seng Khasi is "an association or it includes and stands for all Khasis who follow the tenets and principles of Khasi religion wherever they may be" (Khongphai. 1979:142). Late Sri Jeebon Roy and Sibacharan Roy were the prominent among the founding leaders of the modern *Seng Khasi* movement. The four important principles adopted by Seng Khasi with a view to urgent implementation were (1) adherence to the tenets as specified by the Khasi ancestors, (2) righteousness through service, love and truth(3) respect for one's own fellowmen with humility and faith; and (4) belief in God, the sovereign Lord, the creator and giver of all (Mathur, 1979). The Seng Khasi worked by constituting a number of committees at different levels for the preservation of the Khasi heritage in different fields like education, social welfare, religion, culture, etc. The Seng Khasi movement helped in reinforcing in Khasis the values of their traditional religion and culture to a great extent. Over the years it has outgrown from the status of an association and found people referring to it as if a synonym to that section of the Khasis who follow their traditional religion.

Parallelism and Convergence

Christianity as a religion has strong patrilineal bias and cultural concepts. At the same time matriliny and the cultural complex developed around this matrilineal base is the basic feature of the Khasi social organization. Initially the converts turned away from Khasi culture creating a rift between the converts and the Khasi Khasis (The Khasis who follows the original Khasi religion). The converts were forced to abandon their traditional religious rites, rituals and even festivals and increasingly observed Christian way of celebrations and practises. The animistic way of celebrations associated with funeral ceremonies and ancestor worship were abandoned and they started Christian way of burial. "In the beginning, Christian missionaries spoke against everything native and pagan and, often, one sect spoke against another even during sermons" (Natarajan, 1982:154). It was a Khasi lady, Ka Nabon, she first shown much courage to convert herself to Christianity in 1848 in spite of the stiff resistance from the hands of traditional Khasis. Angell Jones described graphically the hardships and tortures perpetrated on Nabon by the traditional Khasis (Natarajan, 1982). A sense of intolerance was evident not only between traditional Khasis and converts but even between different denominations of Christians both in approach and practise. The cleavage between the Christians and the Khasi Khasis had initially been frequent and bitter and feelings of hatred were mutual. Up on the death of Ka Nabon in 1857, members of her family wanted to cremate her following the traditional Khasi practises. A quarrel and minor revolt ensued. Ultimately Nabon was buried (Natarajan, 1982:157). The missionaries made rules and regulations about the Christian way of life and instructions were given to dissociate with everything native. According to an instance, as reported by Natarajan (1982), a convert of Mowphlang who married a traditional Khasi girl by Khasi rites loosed his membership of the church. Converts to Christianity were even reported to have sold their dance costumes or burnt them (Natarajan, 1982:157). A traditional Khasi farmer was reported to have insisted that Catholic helping hands on his farm must work on Sundays also. It was reported that even in early twentieth century, mutual suspicion and avoidance persisted. "Most issues of the journal U Nongialam Katholic over 1880-1919 were a proof of the animosity between the two groups. Some Christian missionaries had started journals mainly for propagating the message of the church while others were started by Khasi Khasis to express their views which were generally contrary to those of missionaries. Among these are U Naugbit Khupor, Ka Pateng Kristan, U Nougialam Khatholik, U Lurshai, etc. U Khasi Mynta was a Khasi cultural journal" (Natarajan, 1982:154). Early Khasi practises, rituals and practises became symbols of acceptance by the traditionalists and points of rejection by the converts. It was quite evident that the traditional Khasis objected the earlier attempts of Christian missionaries to spread Christianity among them both physically and intellectually. The publication of Khasi cultural journals to counter the Christian missionaries' journal was an example for the resistance at the intellectual level. Whereas the Christian missionaries tried to completely alienate the converts from their traditional culture by framing strict code of conduct for them to observe strictly.

After the initial phase of rift and resistance both the Christian Khasis and Khasi Khasis began to rethink. The Christian missionaries soon realized that their intolerance in the converted Khasis following many of the aspects of their traditional religion including strict adherence to matriliny is not rewarding in attracting more and more Khasis in to their fold. When the missionaries interfered in sacred customs violation of which amounted to a taboo the rate of conversions declined. For example when they encouraged inter kur marriages i.e marriage within members of the same clan (it is unthinkable to a Khasi) the rate of conversions declined in many villages. This has made them to rethink and to tolerate certain degrees of aberrations. On the other hand the children of traditional Khasis were influenced by the western system of education imparted by the Christian missionary institutions opened throughout the Khasi areas especially in and around Shillong. They did not want to close the doors of higher education which is opened before them and enjoyed by their Christian counterparts. They also did not want to restrain the fruits of modern health care facilities facilitated by the Christian missionaries. Both sections of the Khasis were thus confronted with similar problems and compelled to seek solutions. This has ultimately made them to tolerate each other to certain extent bridging their initial phase of rift and resistance. The relatively homogenous ethnic base of the Khasi society to which all the Khasis belonged and the absorptive capacity of the Khasi society facilitated the smooth assimilation while retaining their cultural homogeneity. The corporate nature of the early Khasi life helped them to retain their distinct identity as a unit. Even the Christians found it difficult to break away from this bond. The catholic denomination had adopted a cautious approach from the beginning. They had been practical and tolerant of Khasi culture.

Influx of outsiders in large numbers, leading to varied and more inter-ethnic marriages, upsurge in the economy, greater social capillarity, improvements in the prospects of trade, etc., made them to rose and to adjust to new ways and methods and yet to maintain continuity, what mattered most was being a Khasi, whether Christian or traditional. Their historic experience of exploitation by the outsiders who influxed in to their land during different historical periods had inculcated among them a feeling of insecurity and apprehended that the internal fights would weaken their social solidarity creating scope for outsiders to interfere in their affairs more easily. The Khasis became more unified than ever, wanting to combine the old and the new cultural values, and in their search for a collective identity. Knowledge of a wide horizon has further awakened an in-group consciousness. The plainsmen were looked upon strangers. But the Khasi society was tolerant and accepted an outsider when he took their way of life. Christians accepted some aspects of Khasi culture and traditional Khasis began to emulate the Christians in certain ways for example the way of living.

The Khasis both Christians and non-Christians adjusted themselves in a quick manner to the new cultural and economic environment ushered in by Christianity and western style of education. In some affairs the Christian Khasis found it prudent to come to a compromise with their tribal brethren. For instance the Christian Khasis not only participate but even took a prominent part in the Nongkrem dance festival held at Smith. At the initial stages any Christian Khasi who attended or participated in the traditional dance was liable to excommunicated by the denominational church in which he belonged. The participation of the Christian Khasis in the traditional dances and religious ceremonies is a recent development and tolerated by the Christians without any type of stigma. A number of Muslims from different parts of India and abroad had entered in to marital relations with the Khasis which had led to the growth of a small section of Muslim Khasis the members of which are regarded as Muslims in religion but are, for all other purposes treated as Khasis. The Muslim Khasis –mostly born of Muslim fathers and Khasi mothers have fully retain their tribal heritage. The Khasis both tribal and Christian are keen on preserving their traditional political institutions and associated religious practises.

Nowadays there are a number of socio-cultural institutions formed among the Khasis to reinstate the Khasi solidarity, the memberships in which are given to all irrespective of their religious affiliations. For example the Khasis of Shillong irrespective of their religious association joined hands and formed a number of clan societies for the revitalization of Khasi heritage. It helped to bring all members of the clan together irrespective of the fact that they are Christians or non-Christians. In the gatherings of such associations the clan members belonging to different religious groups never shows any type of intolerance to each other rather they often shows some type of blood ship bonds. But this was not the situation earlier in the initial phase of conversion. Due to the increased communication social events such as marriages, death ceremonies, etc., brought together the relatives together who were otherwise on the polar ends on account of religion. Nowadays no stigma was attached with a Khasi Khasi marrying a Christian

Khasi though they usually try to avoid it. The Christian Khasis in rural areas are found still worshiping the traditional Khasi cult called U Thlen and they also resort to divination during crisis. Many of the first generation Khasis retained some of their old rituals in order to foster the Khasi solidarity. Even though Christianity have made deep inroads in to Khasi religion and culture the Khasis irrespective of their religious faiths still maintain a sentimental attachment in following the traditional customary practises and matrilineal systems. It is this sentimental attachment to their traditional culture that unites them together to identify as a group irrespective of the peripheral differences in the religious identities.

The Sacred Groves

One of the important features of Khasi villages is the presence of forest cover on the margins of the village. Their traditional wisdom helped them to classify the forest into different categories for the purpose of its preservation and management. Associated with each categories of forest there are specific norms and values for its management as well as for its exploitation. This was prominently highlighted through beliefs and customary rights.

One such category of forest is the sacred groves, locally known as *ki lawkyntang*. These groves are considered sacred and contain a variety of plant and tree species. No one was allowed to disturb these groves except for cremation or ritual purposes of the community. They consider disturbing the grove as an offence, which invite supernatural punishment and enforce negative sanctions on the breakers of these traditional norms. These sacred groves play an important role in conserving the bio-diversity of the region. These forests are managed by the *lyngdoh* (community priest) or other persons to whom the religious ceremonies for the particular locality are entrusted. The community for generation preserved the rich forest wealth in the name of religious beliefs which helped them to maintain the ecological balance of the region, ensure water supply, to stop soil erosion in the sloppy terrains and to safeguard the area from air pollution. Approximately about 105.11sq.km of land in the state is under sacred groves (Tiwari, 1997).

Besides sacred forests (*law kyntang*), there are several other types of forest ownerships in the Khasi land such as restricted forests (*law adong*), managed by the Sirdars or headman with the help of village durbar and maintained by the villagers for specific purposes, like firewood for cremation, timber for construction of public buildings like school, meeting hall, etc., There are also clan forests (*law kur*) under the ownership of a particular clan or a group of clans. Maintenance of forest is the collective responsibility of all the families of the clan and the forest produces gained out of it is distributed equally among all its members but those families which did not contribute towards its maintenance were deprived of such benefits (Sarma, 2003). Another category of forest found in the Khasi Hills is the community forests called *law raid* looked after by the *Syiems* or *Durbar Hima*. The produce from this type of the forest is the right of *Syiems or Sirdars* who owns it (Sarma: 2003). There are also forests under private individual ownership known as *law ri-kynti* inherited by families through generations. These forests can be managed and exploited by the respective families as per their desires. In Khasi Hills District, the Autonomous District Council exercises its authority over 95% of the forest area, while the State Government has control on a little over 4%.

To conclude, the Khasis during the last few decades have marched ahead in many respects. Agriculture is still the backbone of Khasi economy but changes are observed in agricultural practices from shifting cultivation to settled agriculture and also from subsistence based agriculture to market oriented agriculture. A middle class is gradually emerging, centered around the urban based occupations and salaried jobs concentrated mainly in Shillong. Christianity has made some deep inroads in to their traditional religion. Along with Christianity, Christian missionaries were also eager to spread education among them and by now education are widespread and Shillong has emerged as a major educational centre in the whole of North-East India. Modern democratic institutions have taken away much of the power and functions of traditional institutions. The pressure from increasing population affected the ecology of the area as well. But there were also revitalization movements to safeguard their traditional religion and to revive the traditional political institutions.

*****

A Break with the Tiffin

A group of Khasi People

Khasi Women in their Traditional Dress

A Khasi family

A Khasi house in a village side

Chapter - III

The Khasi Social Organization

The interaction among members of a society generates social relations. When we speak of social organisation we are referring to the pattern of that interaction. In our effort to study the pattern of such interaction we divide the people of a society into various groups such as family, lineage, clan, etc. In matrilineal societies individuals' initial relationship is to their mother and through her to other kinsmen, both male and female, but continues only through females. The Khasi society is not an exception to such social groupings. It is important to know how these groups are organised in a society and the way the relationships between these groups are defined.

The clan: Structure, Function and Components

Basic to the social organization of the Khasi is the existence of clans called *kur*s. All these clans have specific names. The clan names are used as titles and suffix it with their personal names. All the members of a clan are believed to be descended from a common female ancestor *(ka Iawbei)*. The total number of clans existed among them is not known but Gourdon as early as 1907, has reported about two hundred and three clans in his annexure to the book, "The Khasis" (Reprint in 1975:218-220). But this number might have increased due to the several processes of clan segmentations and clan formation among them. The following forty-seven clans (*kurs*) were found in the Nongrem and Sawmer villages. They are Lyngdoh, Syiem, Warbah, Khyrimujat, Kharngi, Pyngrope, Nongkynrih, Kharbuli, Mylliemngap, Buarban, Kharkonger, Wankhar, Giri, Warkhyttew, Suting, Kharmuti, Nongsteng, Khonglah, Nongstey, Mylloy, Khaabyyar, Nongrum, Shabong, Tron, Jyrwa, Swer, Nongbet, Kharmnuid, Syiemlieh, Marbaniang, Blah, Rani, Khongjee, Wajri, Paswet, Lyngwa, Sun, Thankiew,

Nongtraw, Dkhar, Majaw, Deingdoh, Mawthoh, Kharshiing, Hynniewta, Kharmaphlang, and Synrem. A clan may branch out in different groups and adopt different names and thus new clans may arise. New clans may also develop due to other process as well. The clans are matrilineal in descent and strictly exogamous in character. Breaking of rule of clan exogamy was punished by excommunication in the past. Even now such sanctions are imposed on the offenders. But no such cases were reported among them in the recent past as they strictly adhere to such strictures. For the culprits a funeral ceremony at death was refused and his/her bones were not allowed to keep in the sepulchre of the clan. This practise of keeping the bones in cairns has now been abandoned due to several reasons. One reason is the large scale conversion to other faiths like Christianity and Islam and the consequent changes in funeral practises.

In this respect it is worth while to quote Rymbai (1974): "persons guilty of the sacrilege are outcasted…the outcasted are not only disowned and dispossessed, but are also denied the solace of religion. No religious rite or ceremony can be performed for them, and when they die their ashes have no place in the Cairns of the kurs" (Quoted in Chowdhury 1996:207).

It is also worth to quote Kynpham Singh in this regard. "In ancient times, those who indulged in intra-clan illicit sexual relationship were stigmatised and driven not only from the clan but from the Khasi community and they inevitably got lost among other races and tribes" (Quoted in Chowdhury 1996:207). Even though a majority of them have embraced Christianity they are still found observing the rule of clan exogamy as persistently as possible as in the past notwithstanding their religious affinities. Even the Christian churches have established a *komity sang* (taboo committee) to look into dubious cases referred to it.

A Khasi, whether male or female, adopts the title of his/her mother and suffix it with his/her personal names. The titles are always the name of their *kurs* or clans. Thus Victor the son of Mary belonging to the Kharbuli clan is called Victor Kharbuli and Victor's sister Elizabath is called Elizabath Kharbuli. Birth determines one's title. It will not change after marriage. Khasis do not adopt father's title as it would possibly disrupt the principle of clan exogamy on which the whole social fabric of the community was woven around. The reason is that adoption of fathers' titles may lead to marriages between clan members unwittingly, which they considered to be a taboo and the greatest sin a Khasi can ever commit. The practice of adopting father's title has become a style at least among those who live outside the Khasi domain to cope with the practise there but as soon as they come back to the Khasi fold they reverts to tradition. The English style of using Mr and Mrs so and so is not a correct usage as far as the Khasis are concerned. In few cases some ladies working outside Meghalaya are found adopted such a style. But these are rare cases followed out of compulsion to suit to such situation and the Khasis never intend to break the tradition as it might lead to the danger of marriage with blood relatives.

The clans are found scattered across the villages and the spread of a clan is not confined to a locality or geographical area. A clan generally have a wider geographical spread. Several clans are found in a village. A clan did not have any specific leader and the clan members hardly have a social occasion to come together and meet. The interaction between clan members was limited and a Khasi's knowledge about his clansmen residing outside his village is little and limited. A Khasi will be more familiar with his own village men though they are distinctly related and are members of different clans than his own clansmen residing outside the village. Since most of the marriages were within the village/locality, a majority of the villagers would be related to each other either consanguineally or affinally. Nowadays most of the clans have constituted its own clan councils known as *kur durbars* with an elected headman called *Rangbah kur* and other office bearers. The adult male members of the clan elect the most influential male member of the clan as the headman. Traditionally it was the *Rangbah kur* he who allocated the land for cultivation and other human activities like building houses, etc., among its members. The most important function of the *kur* among the Khasis today is regulation of marriage between blood relatives.

The clans among the Khasis are not totemic. But there are some clans the members of which maintains certain type of relationship with certain birds, animals or objects with which they were believed to have certain associations. For example, members of Kharumnuid clan do not take pork and they even do not allow anyone to carry them in their vehicles. They also do not encourage their clansmen to rear them.

Some of the clans derived their names from trees, animals, and birds and or from some natural objects. For example, the Deingdoh clan derived its name from *deingdoh* tree; *Shrieh* is the name of another clan, which means monkey in Khasi language. Similarly *Tham* meaning crab is also a clan name. The members of these clans do not consider these trees or animals as totems nor do they abstain from killing or eating them.

Clan Segmentation and Emergence of New Clans

There are different processes of clan *(kur)* segmentation and formation of new clans among the Khasis. The following cases describe few such processes of new clan formations.

The traditional process of clan segmentation: The members of a particular clan (*kur)* have a common *mauba*. This is a gravestone wherein the bones of all the dead members are collected and buried. When a *mauba* becomes full they create another branch *mauba* and the original *kur* branches out and forms a new *kur* and adopts a new name. This is the traditional process of clan segmentation and formation of new clans among them. Thus the *kurs* branched out from the same major *kur* are considered as sister *kurs (shi kur)* and hence its members are not allowed to intermarry. At the time of marriage it has to be verified whether the boy and the girl belong to the same *kur* or to two different *kurs* that had branched out from the same stem in the past. If found the clans had branched out from the same clan, their marriages were not permitted.

This practise of keeping bones of the deceased clan members in the Cairns is becoming obsolete at least among Christian Khasis. Since the Christian Khasis has abandoned the practice of cremation of the dead and adopted burial there is no scope to observe this practice any more. Hence many of the rites and rituals associated with cremation were also gradually disappeared. Nowadays even the Khasi Khasis (Khasis who follows their traditional Khasi religion) prefer burial to cremation due to the scarcity of firewood.

Marriage with a non-Khasi girl by a Khasi boy: Marriage with non-Khasi girls by Khasi boys often ends in the formation of new clans. Since the Khasis follow strict matriliny they cannot adopt the clan names of their father and also cannot adopt the clan name of their mother since she is an outsider (*Dkhar*). In this situation, they have no other option but to form a new clan. If the number of marriages with non-Khasi girls increases the number of clans among the Khasis will also be on the increase. All the Khasi clans with a prefix of *Khar* are thus originated. *Dkhar* in their language means 'outsider' and *Khar* is an abbreviated form of *Dkhar.*

The origin of *Kharpyngrope* clan is a typical example for this process of clan formation. A man of *Pyngrope* clan married a Nepali girl and for their children they created a new clan, *Kharpyngrope,* prefixing *Khar* to his original clan *Pyngrope*. One Torist Syiem, who married a Nepali girl adopted the title G*iri* as a new clan for his children. Contrary to the tradition of prefixing the term 'Khar' to clans thus originates, Torist just adopted the name 'Giri'. As the Khasis do not have any prohibitions in marrying an outsider the number of such clans will be on increase, whereas marriage with a non-Khasi man by a Khasi girl does not result in such a situation since the children can adopt mothers' title. In Khasi-Garo intermarriages, the children are found adopting mother's title. As the two communities are matrilineal this does not pose any problem as far as the clan affiliation of the children is concerned.

Other process such as deliberate segregation by individual members on various grounds: One Jefry Kharbuli originated the clan Diengkseh. Jefry was a young enthusiastic man, married a girl from a Lyngdoh clan. He himself belonged to the Kharbuli clan as his title indicates. He, contrary to the Khasi tradition, wanted to give his title to his wife and children and in this respect submitted a request to the *durbar kur kharbuli* (Kharbuli clan committee). But the *durbar kur kharbuli* readily rejected the plea seeing that it is against the Khasi tradition. Agitated by the decision of the *durbar* Jefry formed a new clan named *Diengkseh*. Jefry's wife and children and their children in the female line of descent belong to this clan.Thus the number of clans among the Khasis is not fixed and new clans may arise every now and then due to this various process of clan segmentation and formation.

Clan Hierarchies and Marriageable Clans

There are no superior/ inferior clans or clan hierarchies among the Khasis. Even then the Syiem and Lyngdoh clans always have a functional importance since they are the royal and priestly clans respectively. The title of the children is always that of their mothers. Hence the children born to Syiem man cannot enjoy the prevalence and privileges associated with the title of their father. But they have a privilege to add the title *giri* before their real title. For example Courstar, son of a Syiem man and Kharbuli woman will be known as Courstar Giri Kharbuli signifying that he is son of a Syiem man. But this *giri* term is now used to name a new clan as discussed above. Such tradition of adopting the second title to signify the fathers' clan is not in practise in the case of Lyngdoh clan.

There are no clan preferences in marriage. Though the clans beginning with 'Khar" signifies that they are not pure clans, they originated out of Khasi-non-Khasi marriages they have not been looked down for any purposes on that ground. Same way there is no preferences in getting married from the royal and priestly clans (Syiem and Lyngdoh) due to their higher functional status. Paying of bride price or dowry was not in practice and marriage among them was a simple affair. Those who break the rule of clan exogamy were ostracized in the past.

Clan interconnectedness has various social dimensions. For example, the following clans do not intermarry. They are Lyngdoh, Mawthoh, Lyngbah, Pongrup, Khynriem Mawshorok, Nonghulew and Khonglitung, because they are considered as sister clans (*shi kur*). So is the case of Thankiew clan, as they do not marry with Blah, Shylla and Pariat clans. There are other instances of clans being connected with one another. Such connections are being called *iatch kur*. For example the members of the Lyngdoh clan cannot intermarry Kharmoti clan not because they are descendents from the same mother but they believe that the ancestress mother of the Kharmoti clan was an orphan and grown up by a Lyngdoh and hence treated to be equal to a sister. Among the Thankiew clan, there are two divisions: Laikpoh and Shikpoh. Intermarriages between them, though not prohibited, normally do not take place. The story of the origin of two divisions among them tells like this: the Laikpoh Thankiew was the original clan; there was a servant girl with one of the Thankiew mothers and she was very loyal. She loved her as if she was her own daughter and later she has given even her title to her and it is her descendents are known as Shikpoh Thankiew.

Though a majority of the Khasis in the studied villages are Christian no basic changes are visible in the structural organisation of the community. The rule of clan exogamy is observed as strictly as it was in the past. But, though not strong, elements of change in several aspects of the matrilineal system are observable. Generally Khasis will not agree in changing and adopting the title of the father which they believe will end in incest, i.e. marriage between blood relatives. In other aspects such as residence and inheritance of property many of them believe that changes need to happen and its signs are already been visible. It is a fact that in several aspects of their culture they are gradually discarding many customs and habits without observing them as steadfastly as in the past or are just neglecting without observing them with due regard. For example, the shift from cremation to burial both among Christian Khasis and Khasi Khasis but on different grounds have made obsolete the practise of collection of bones and its deposit in a common cairn and the latter erecting of monoliths and a series of rituals and observances associated with each such ritual. The world view which comprises the religious beliefs and practices, the idea of supernatural, etc., of a society has a tendency to endure and resist changes even in a situation of culture contact. But among the Khasis, especially among the Christian Khasis, changes are being observed even on these aspects of culture.

Lineage

The structural organization of Khasis is woven around two institutions, i.e. the *kpoh* and the *iing*. The *kpoh* of the Khasi is more or less equivalent to the English word 'lineage'. The *kpoh* contains descendents of three or four generations tracing descent from one great grand mother. The descent is reckoned strictly on the matrilineal line eliminating the wife and children

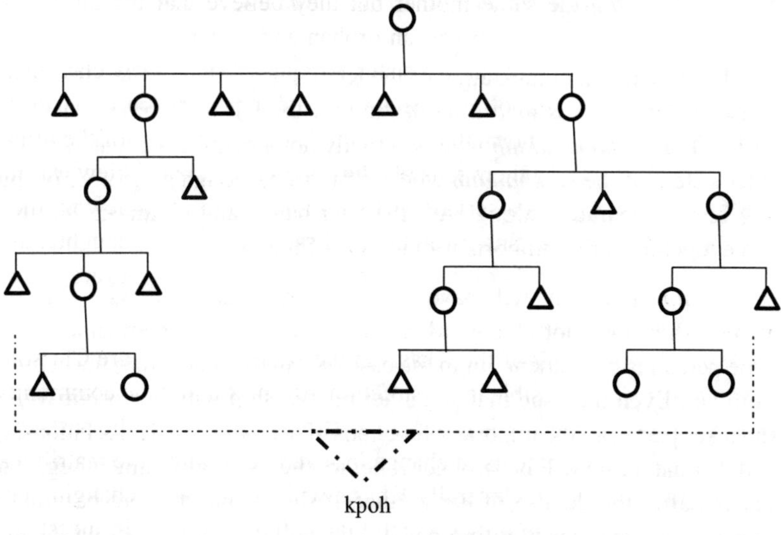

Diagram - II: Composition of the* kpoh *organization of the Khasis.

of male members and husbands of female members. Beyond that, relationships are recognised as being a part of a *kur* who at one point of time were closely related. Nakane (1961) has defined the *kpoh* organization of Khasis as "a group of matrilineal kins usually confined to one domestic family or groups of households linked by direct extension of the main household". A member of a *kpoh* will be living, especially a male member, away from the main household, i.e. the household of the great grand mother from whom descent is being reckoned. The *kpoh* organization of Khasis is not functional as its members hardly come together for a social cause.

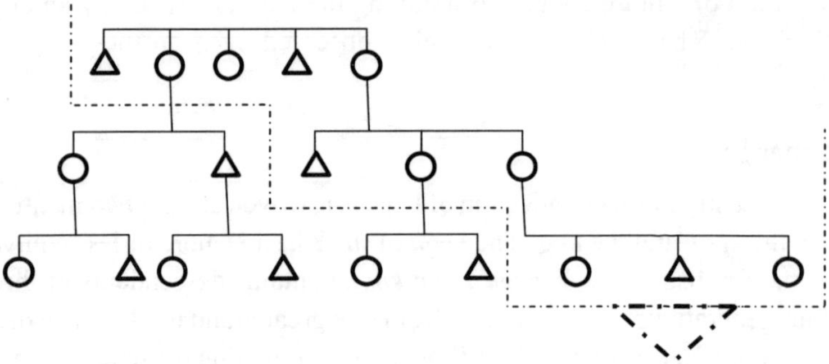

Digram - II: Functional Composition of the iing.

The functional organization of the Khasis is the *iing*. It literally means house or family. It is also a domestic unit though it accommodates the husband of the *ka khadduh* who is actually not a member of that *iing*. The elder sisters of the *ka khadduh* who are married, though a member of that *iing* reside separately along with their husbands and children. But they come together for all important functions of the *iing*.

An *iing* normally will have only three generations depth. The *iing* membership does not change after marriage. The *iing* membership of a male person is permanent but in the case of females a new *iing* may sprout from her. Even then she maintains her relationship with her original *iing* and takes part in all the important functions of her natal *iing*. Her relationship with her natal *iing* will be stronger if her mother were alive and it begins to slacken after the demise of her mother. It shows that the *iing* has only a narrow range and never accommodates the collateral relatives and it splits up and forms new *iings* by every daughter of a mother. For some time a female may have a dual membership of *iing*, one in which she was born and the other is one, which originated from her. She and her children belong to the newly formed *iing* by her but her husband even though a co-resident is not a member in that *iing*.

Thus the *kpoh* is a maximal lineage and the *iing* is a minimal lineage. But none of these institutions of the Khasi is a property group. The members of a particular clan do not have a collective ownership over the clan land. It is owned by *ka khadduhs* of different lines and managed by their maternal uncles.

Though the members of an *iing* do not have a collective ownership over the land, it is the responsibility of the *ka khadduh* who inherits and owns the ancestral property to arrange all the important family functions including the arrangement of marriages of its members and all the important religious rituals of the family. If a brother is coming back home after divorce, separation or being widowed, the *khadduh* has to readily accept him and normally she will do it very happily. If the children of an elder sister become destitute after the death of their mother and their father being remarried to another lady, the *khadduh* has to take the responsibility of looking after them. Thus the *iing* though not a property group have to take certain responsibilities for the well being of its members.

Family

Generally two types of families are found among the Khasis, the nuclear and the extended. Daughters other than the *ka khadduh* establish the nuclear families after marriage. A mother, if it is affordable to her, may demarcate a small plot of land to build a house for her elder daughters. If the mother is financially sound she may also help them in building a house as well but it is not obligatory. If the wife's family is not economically sound enough to do so the husband and wife have to pool their earnings and have to buy a plot of land to build a house. Several families are found staying in rented houses and are unable to make a house of their own due to their poor economic conditions.

The extended houses are the houses of *ka khadduhs*. Different combinations of members are found in such extended houses. It may comprise the *khadduh* and her family, her unmarried sisters and brothers, her remaining parents, divorced or deserted or widowed brothers and the children of her deceased sisters or a different combination of all these relatives.

Seven families out of the 150 households surveyed are found living patrilocally i.e., husband, wife, and their children living along with husband's parents in their residence. Sometimes the nuclear family may be added with the wife's mother and her maternal uncle and their children. In some cases it was found the mother, her husband and children and her children in her earlier marriage all living together. Since divorce and remarriages are common this combination of members in a family is not rare. If a lady gets divorced or husband deceased, she may get remarried and she would continue to keep her children of her earlier marriage with her and thus this type of family arises. In some other cases, it was found, the unmarried elder sisters continue to live along with the *khadduh* sister and her family.

The *khadduh*'s house is the pivot of activities frequented by both brothers and uncles alike. Important family crises and other matters are discussed and resolved. Uncle is the counsellor and guardian of his sister's children. The uncle is always at hand in case of hard times. If the father fails or become irresponsible it is the maternal uncle who has to step in to his shoes.

The Khasi male has a dual role to play as an uncle in his own *iing* and as a father to his own children. The eldest brother or son of each house through each generation is entrusted with responsibility of being a kind of priest of that particular house. The responsibility is handed down and taught by his elder maternal uncles. He undertakes the duty of performing the necessary religious rites within his household. As he is not a real Lyngdoh or priest these rites pertain only to the well being of his family. In matters relating to family properties and affairs concerning other close members of the clan the *khadduh* refers them to her elder brothers and uncles.

The Khasis are found to be reluctant to adopt family planning techniques. The Khasi families have an average of seven children. The highest number of children being observed was eighteen out of which six had deceased and the remaining twelve survives. The infant mortality rate is also high among the Khasis. Early marriages and their reluctance to adopt family planning methods are found to be the major reason for the high birth rates among them.

The female members of a family though married and set up their own household but would get daily opportunities to come together owing to the matrilocal residence and matrilineal inheritance pattern prevalent among them. During their leisure hours, the sisters, both direct and maternal cousin sisters, come together, chitchat and share the *kowai* (pan and betel nuts). The pattern of residence after marriage makes it possible for them to have such gathering as they will be living in the adjoining lands demarcated for them by their mothers. This would help in reinforcing in them a feeling of oneness. At the same time their male counterparts hardly get an occasion like this to come together and meet. This is because of the matrilocal residence rule followed by the community. Brothers after marriage normally settle in their wife's places, which would be at a distance to each other.

Marriage

Girls feel that what they are looking for while considering a boy for alliance is his conduct and character, i.e. the ability to conduct the family responsibly and his educational status, job, the social background of the family, etc. Many of the girls who are well educated and many among them employed as well even after the age of twenty-five or more are found remain unmarried in both the villages. They found difficulty in getting proper mates of their choice with education and job equal to them. As far as education and job were concerned a man falls in the category of underachievers compared to women and hence they are not preferred by educated and employed girls. Handsomeness is always a matter of secondary consideration. Traditionally the economic background of the family of a boy was overlooked while seeking alliance in a matrilineal society, like that of Khasis where inheritance of property is strictly in the female line. Whatever be the economic background of the boy he cannot inherit anything and he has to fend for himself. But recently changes could be observed in this mentality and many share the view that the economic background of a boy's family is also an important aspect to be considered while seeking alliances especially in the cases of arranged marriages.

Some of the boys feel that it is better to prefer a *khaddduh* for marriage, as it will ensure the financial security of the family. Whereas some others are of the view that choosing a *khadduh* for marriage is non-prolific, as it will hamper the charm and beauty of family life as the position of being the husband of a *khadduh* (i.e.*padduh*) is stressful enough to spoil the peace of mind. The couple cannot start an independent life as long as the parents of the *khadduh* survive and her siblings get married. Even after that the wife has to shoulder several responsibilities as a *khadduh* and have to face several crises. She can never be fully devoted to her husband and children, as she also has to fulfil her commitments to her *iing* being the legal heiress of the property of the family. It is evident that the taste and preferences in marriage differ from person to person.

Some of the informants pointed out that besides considering the beauty and family status of the girls' family, they also verify before marriage whether the girl's family is the secret worshipers of the *thlen* or not. The Khasi people still hold their belief in *thlen* (There is a long story associated with *thlen* in the folk beliefs of the Khasis). *Thlen* is a gigantic snake that takes abode secretly in some of the Khasi houses and the worshipper of it would become prosperous but the only condition is that it should be propitiated by offering blood by human sacrifice. People believe that association with such families may spoil the good name of their family and it may harm their life itself as the possibility of being sacrificed to offer blood to *thlen* cannot be discarded.

Ninety two percent of the marriages in the sample survey are love marriages. Love marriages are of two types. In the first type, the parents of the parties, after coming to know that they were in love, arranged the marriage. In such cases some sort of rituals were to be observed. The other type of marriage was secretive in character, the girl and the boy lived like husband and wife for sometimes without the notice of others and once it came to known by others their relatives arrange their marriage without any ritual. In such cases the society would not normally impose any sort of sanctions on them and accept them as husband and wife provided that the rule of clan exogamy is not broken.

Marriage outside the community is not usually objected to but they do not encourage such marriages. If the community come to know about such possibility of marriage with an outsider before hand they try to discourage him or her from such alliance. No stigma is attached towards the children born out of inter-community marriages. The number of marriages between Khasi girls and non-Khasi boys were more than the marriages between Khasi boys and non-Khasi girls.

Table 7: Inter Religious and Inter Community Marriages.

Type of Marriage	*No. of Marriages (Nongkrem)*	*No. of Marriages (Sawmer)*	*Total*
Khasi Khasis with Christian Khasis	3	3	6
Khasis with Non- Khasis	5	11	16
Khasis with Muslims	0	3	3
With other sub-groups	2	9	11
Total	**10**	**26**	**36**

Source: Fieldwork

No stigma was attached with a Khasi Khasi marrying a Christian Khasi though they usually try to avoid it. During the survey only six such cases were reported. In sixteen cases they are married with non- Khasis. It consisted of Garos (5), Nepalis (7), Karbi (1), Anglo-Indian (1), and Mizo (1). In three cases the Khasi girls have married Muslim boys and in eleven cases the marriage is between different sub groups of Khasis. Rest of the marriages are with in the same ethnic and religious group.

Before the marriage the choice has to be carefully screened for keeping the clan sanctity. Following a personal choice, the first move for the marriage proposal comes from the boy's side with the approval of his maternal uncle as well as the relatives of his father. In the first instance, there is an elaborate examination about *sang* (taboo), family background and so on by the representatives of the two *kurs* (clans). Older maternal uncles or any chosen go-between ask for the girls hand in marriage on behalf of the boy. If there is no bar to their marriage, then follows the betrothal ceremony and presenting of rings. Females from the boy's side are not allowed to attend the function, which takes place in the girl's house. A broken engagement is considered as *klim ka synjat* (adultery over the engagement), which breaks a covenant in the eyes of god.

The marriage day is marked by the exchange of betel nuts between the boy's party and the welcoming party of the bride accompanied by the beating of drums, dance and music. Again the female members of the boy's side are not allowed to attend. It is usually a practice that the females of the boy's side can visit the girl's house only after the newly weds have visited the mother-in-law of the girl.

Divorces among the Khasis are common and do not involve much rituals and complications but it often takes place on mutual consent. Divorce is not generally allowed during pregnancy and once separated cannot remarry afterwards. The husband and wife after a quarrel may separate for sometimes without observing the coin ceremony and this type of separation is called *shongkhlad.* It does not have the legal sanction. The legal separation involves the observation of coin ceremony in which, in the presence of friends and relatives of both the parties, the husband and wife bring five coins each. The wife gives her coins to her husband and he in turn gives back ten coins adding his five. She returns them to him again and he throws them on the ground. Observance of this ritual gives the legal sanction to the divorce. A crier goes around the village and announces the divorce. This type of divorce is known as *sanshyieng.* Poverty, joblessness and irresponsibility, being the male characteristics, considered to be the important reasons for the high rate of divorce among the Khasis. Early marriages are said to be another reason for the breakage of many marital relations among them.

There is no custom of hypergamy as there are no superior-inferior considerations among the clans and also among the sub-groups. The Khasi community is also endogamous. Conversion to Christianity does not create any stigma and nowadays marriage between Khasi Khasis and Christian Khasis are taking place. Six cases of such marriages were reported in the survey.

The Khasis practice monogamy, i.e. only one partner at a time. There is no taboo in remarrying once the previous partner has died or divorced. Neither polyandry nor polygyny existed among them. A Khasi can not marry two sisters at a time but one can marry his deceased wife's younger sister (junior sorrorate) after the expiry of one year from wife's death on payment of *iing sang* (price of *sang* or taboo) to the wife's clan. There is no taboo in marrying one's deceased sister's elder sister (senior sorrorate) also but as a matter of fact it seldom takes place. Marrying deceased husband's brother, elder or younger (senior and junior levirate), is not prohibited but no such case was reported in the study.

As a rule there was no prohibition in marrying mother's brother's daughter since they belong to two different clans. But they have an inherent antipathy to such marriages. It was told that there is no harm in marrying mother's brother's daughter after the death of the mother's brother (maternal uncle) but cannot be done when he is alive. Normally they avoid it if they are first-degree relatives and approve if the relations are distant. Parallel cousin marriages (whether maternal or paternal) are prohibited and considered as a sin. Even though the paternal cousins always belong to two different clans, they are marriageable from the point of view of clan exogamy but it is prohibited among the Khasis. They have specific terms for this prohibited degree of marriages: the marriage between sisters' children is known as *parakha* and the marriage between brothers' children is known as *bakha.* Marriage with the daughter of a paternal aunt (FZD) is discouraged even though they belong to two different clans. These types of marriages amount to a taboo called ai *khaw kylliang*, which is an insult to the father because it means a return of bread and luck.

Marriage by exchange is prohibited. But two brothers can marry two sisters though it is quite uncommon. But one condition to be fulfilled is that the elder brother has to marry the elder sister and the younger brother marries the younger sister and not vice versa.

Though there are no clan preferences in marriages, there are some clans, members of which do not intermarry. For example, the people belonging to Lyngdoh and Pyngrope do not intermarry. Likewise marriages between members of Warbah, Warshong, Suting and Warkhylew are also prohibited.

One important feature of Khasi marriages, observed during the survey was that a majority of the marriages has taken place within the village/ locality. Because of this tendency of village endogamy most of the members of the village are linked to each other, either affinally or consanguineally. From childhood days itself, the boys and girls develop some sort of intimacy between them and later on that may develop into a love affair and they get married. This is one of the main reasons for the endogamous marriages within the limits of a village. Even on such occasions the partners would be very much conscious of the clan identity of the other as the socialising process reinforces in them the danger involved in marrying a girl or boy of his/her own group

Table 8: Patterns of Marriage.

Marital Patterns	*No. of Marriages (Nongkrem)*	*No. of Marriages (Sawmer)*	*Total*
Inside the Locality	10	41	51
Inside the Village	50	17	67
Outside the Village	4	91	95
Total	**64**	**149**	**213**

Source: Fieldwork

Out of a total of two hundred and thirteen marriages, sixty-seven were outside the locality but within the village. Fifty-one marriages have taken place within the locality and ninety-five outside the village. There was a considerable difference in the number of 'marriages outside the village' between two villages selected for the study. This is mainly because compared to Nongkrem, which consists of eleven localities, the Sawmer village is small in its geographical area and consists only four localities only and hence the scope for choice of mates within the village will be less. Another reason is that since the Sawmer is in a semi-urban setting and having better communication facilities the scope for interaction with people of other villages is high.

No evidence of existence of polyandry was found in both the studied villages. But Chi Nakane (1967) has reported the existence of polyandry in two of the villages she had studied by about four decades back. They do not posses more than one husband, at least, at a time. They may marry more than one not at a time but serially. But the strict strictures by the churches have helped in bringing down the number of divorces among the Christian Khasis. Catholics allow remarriages only on the death of first wife/husband but its Presbyterian counterpart allows divorce on strong grounds.

Matriliny assures that every child born is legitimate because it belongs to the clan *(kur)* of its mother. In a society where divorce is common and frequent, there is every possibility for the children being neglected and become destitute. The Khasi society has its own mechanisms to sort out such casualties. It is a fact that the number of marriages between Khasi women and non-Khasi men are several fold more than the number of marriages between Khasi men and non-Khasi women. The community members have given several explanations for this trend. One reason is that the property of the Khasi is inherited through the female line and hence those who have an eye on their properties try to entice the ladies and marry them. Another reason being given is that the Khasi men generally fall under the category of non-achievers and hence the non-Khasis seldom feel comfortable in marrying them. Whatever may be the reason for this trend, it was observed that most of the non-Khasi men after a brief period of married life and after getting one or more children deserted their wives and disappear from the scene and in most cases the mothers were found getting remarried. Under such a situation, it is obvious that there may be an influx of orphans in such a community. But in Khasi society, nobody is an orphan since the matrilineal system takes care of the children whether an orphan, divorcee, deserted or whatever it is. It is a fact that even in a city like Shillong one can hardly find a Khasi destitute in its streets contrary to the other cities of the country. This is because the matrilineal system prevalent among them ensures that no one in that society is born as an orphan: every child is a legitimate member of his or her clan.

Residence

Residence after marriage among the Khasis is either matrilocal or neolocal. In case of marriage of daughters, other than the youngest, the pattern of residence is neolocal. But in the initial years of their marriage until they build a house of their own, they stay matrilocally. Once they find the couple is going well together they establish their own household. In case of the youngest daughter i.e., *ka khadduh*, she and her husband and children continue to live in her mother's residence and she inherits it on her mother's demise.

Table 9: Patterns of Residence.

Residence type	*No. of families*
Matrilocal	45
Patrilocal	6
Neolocal	49
Total	**100**

Source: Fieldwork

Out of the hundred families surveyed in the Sawmer village 49% were neolocal and 45% matrilocal. Six percent of them are following patrilocal residence pattern. Out of a total of forty-nine neolocal families, twenty five of them got lands from the wife's parents to build houses and for eight families land was provided by husband's parents. Rest of them are either living in rented houses or in houses built by them by their own savings.

In some cases, the wives were found staying in the residences of their husbands since they have no sisters to look after the family property. As per tradition such residences at any reason cannot continue beyond the death of their husbands. After the demise of their husbands the wives and their children have to leave the house giving space to their deceased husbands' maternal relatives (mother's sister's youngest daughter) to occupy it. People have deliberately found a way out in such a situation. Before the death of the husband they manage to get the property registered it in the name of their children. A man after the death of his wife goes back to his natal home if his deceased wife is a *khadduh* and her parents are still alive and some of her unmarried siblings are still living there. If his children alone are there he may continue to stay there his rest of life. But if he is remarrying he has to shift to his new in-law's house.

Nakane (1967) has pointed out that duolocal residence existed among them till recent past and that the practice of village endogamy suited duolocal residence. But in the studied villages 55% of the marriages were village/ locality endogamous but not a single case of duolocal residence was reported.

A man though lives with the wife's relatives, his ashes after death can find no place within the wife's family tomb. His wife and children can cremate the dead body but the bone and ashes has to be handed over to his maternal relatives to deposit in their *kur* cairn through a prolonged ritual. But in the case of death of community Lyngdoh (priest), his wife and children cannot cremate his dead body. It has to be handed over to his maternal relatives for cremation. As more and more Khasis embraced Christian faith and cremation is becoming obsolete, these rituals have also declined.

Among the Khasis two women belonging to two different descent groups never reside together. A man and his wife never lived together with his sister. In one rare case, a man was found staying in his ancestral house along with his wife and sister. But it is told that this is only a temporary arrangement to help his sister, as his sister was still unmarried and since there was nobody else to help her out, he and his family live with her. They have to move out once she got married.

Inheritance and Succession

Regarding property, the youngest daughter (*ka khadduh*) inherits the house and the major share of landed properties, as she has the social responsibility to look after the aged parents, widowed sisters and brothers and orphaned nephews and nieces. The custodianship of the family jewellery rested with her to be transferred to the following generation. She has a special role to play as a custodian of family property and as a central pivot in whose house all family, social, kinship, and religious activities are performed. If the youngest daughter dies the youngest among the surviving daughters inherited the property and the social role. Other daughters may also inherit a plot of land for their house sites depending upon the economic condition of the family. They may also be helped financially by their parents to build a house of their own if they could afford. In some cases the male members inherited lands and house of their mothers. Contrary to their customary laws, in some exceptional cases the daughterless mothers gave their landed property to their sons. Many of the respondents shared their feeling that some basic changes needed in the system of inheritance of property and male members also have to get a share of the property.

Customarily, in the event of youngest daughter changing her religion, or committing an act of *sang* or taboo, she lost her position in the family and was succeeded by the youngest in the line of sisters as in the case of death. But now a days as more and more Khasis are being embraced Christianity change of religion is not considered as an act of *sang* and hence is often tolerated and overlooked.

The *ka khadduh* is entitled to get largest share of the landed property on account of her religious and family duties. Her main religious duty is to perform the cremation of her mother and deposit the bones of all the members of her family in their final resting place under a megalithic stone (*Mawbah*) (Erection of megalithic stones is no more in practise in the two studied villages). It is also obligatory on her part to feed the invalid and the non-earning members of the family. The Christian *ka khadduhs* do not perform the traditional religious ceremonies but still follow the traditional system of inheritance pattern.

The maternal uncle shows a keen interest in the management of family property. The institution of *ka khadduh* is vulnerable. Mismanagement, abuse or loss of property can pose a serious threat to the economic stability and continuity of the matrilineal group. This is where the role of the maternal uncle can be positive. The maternal kin imposes its own sanctions on non-conforming members and in a close-knit society like that of the Khasis it is a powerful social force.

In the absence of a female child, the ancestral property will go to the mother's sister's *khadduuh* daughter and not to her sons. Her sons can live and enjoy their mothers' family property as long as they live and after their death, the property will go to their maternal parallel cousin sisters and never to their wife and children, male or female. There were several such instances in the Nongkrem village. This is one of the main reasons why the parents preferred female to male children. It checked the alienation of ancestral property to the hands of some other relatives than their own children. There are several instances in which sons selling out the property of the female issueless mothers with the silent consent of their cousin sisters who were supposed to be the future heiress of such properties. Both the parties benefited by such a deal, the future heiress otherwise had to wait for years for the property to come her way, until the death of all the sons of the owner of the property as they could enjoy it as long as they lived. It may even not take place during her lifetime. By selling it they avoided the uncertainty involved in it. If the khaddduh did not have a female issue the property will go to other maternal relatives and never to her sons. By joining hands with her cousin brothers both the parties benefited and they use that money to purchase other properties which they can give to their sons if they wished, as it would fall under the category of earned property (*nongkhynraw).* Now a days the parents are using different tactics to give even the inherited landed properties to their sons in the absence of daughters.

All the properties acquired by a man before marriage goes to his mother and will be inherited by his youngest sister. The properties that he earns after the marriage go to his wife and children and later, would be inherited by his youngest daughter. It is a fact that when a man purchased a plot of land by his hard earned money he often get it registered in the name of his wife and not in his own name.

Table 10: Pattern of Registration of land.

Pattern of registration	*No. of cases (Nongkrem)*	*No. of cases (Sawmer)*	*Total*
In the name of husband	8	15	23
In the name of wife	12	6	18
Total	20	21	41

Source: Fieldwork

In Nongkrem village out of the twenty samples of land registration twelve were in the name of wives and only eight in husbands' names. Sawmer village give a different picture where out of 21 cases 15 are registered in the name husband and the remaining six in wife's names.

The following two cases from Nongrem village prove that the mothers these days prefer to give a share of their property to their male children, as well if they can afford. The mother of the present headman of the Warbah has four children, three sons and a daughter. In her case, she has divided all her property among her children including boys but of course a little more to her daughter. She also built four houses one each for her children. In this case, the headman's wife who is also a *khadduuh*, contrary to the tradition, came and stayed with him instead of him going and joining her relatives. More interestingly, his wife's mother, who is also a *khadduh,* is coming and staying in her daughter's husband's residence leaving her aged mother under the custody of some other maternal relatives.

In yet another case, one mother has given about two acres of land to her son, which is very uncommon among the Khasis. Though he has three brothers and a sister, his mother in this way favoured none other than him. The rest of the property was given to his lone sister. The Khasi mother justified this in this way; since he married a Nepali girl he would not be availing any property or financial assistance from his in-laws. Hence he has to mend by himself. In the case of other sons they will go and stay with their in-laws after marriage and will get assistance from them.

The Sawmer village originally belong to the Kharkonger clan. If the inheritance is strictly on the female line and not transferable, there should have been only Kharkonger people in that village except the in-married males. But the settlement pattern and ownership of landed property proves differently.

Traditionally the *khadduhs* cannot sell the ancestral property without the consent of the other matrilineal members and that also in acute necessity. This pattern is now undergoing change. Once married a Khasi man is not obliged to return his self-acquired property to his natal home. Although in some cases, he does so if his relation with his wife is strained.

Chi Nakane (1967:105) surmised that the rule of female ultimogeniture succession might have developed in conjunction with the shortage of land. She assumed that since the plot of land is just enough to maintain one household, the youngest daughter holds the title to it when it passes on to next generation and this fact leads to exclude married elder daughters from the right to use the land. The rule of ultimogeniture inheritance of property creates inbalance in the economy. In many cases it is observed that the *khadduh* sister and her family, living in good houses and enjoying landed properties, while their sisters living in rented or poor houses and engaging in hard labour to earn their livelihood.

Traditionally, the youngest daughter (*ka khadduh*) was only the custodian of family or clan property, family jewellery, and the ancestral home, which are managed and controlled by her maternal uncles or in their absence her elder brothers. She also had to take the responsibility of looking after the aged parents or any other member of the family during distress. It is reported that the extension of British rule to the region resulted in the misinterpretation of this very system and the customary role has increased beyond custodianship to a legal heiress.

The matrilineal system among the Khasis is not continuing unchallenged, though it may look calm from outside, it is internally turbulent. There is a section among them which are not satisfied with the sort of affair prevailing with in the system. Though isolated, the attempts to change the system are more than four decades old. An organisation called *Ka seng Iktiar Longbriew Manbriew* was formed in 1961 to spearhead a movement for change in the matrilineal system in favour of patriliny especially in the matters of descent, inheritance and succession. The organisation with this objective continued their activities but could not make much headway. The State Government in 1980's requested its Law Commission to draft a Bill enabling the parents to bequeath their self-acquired property to distribute among their children as per their wish. The Law Commission prepared a Bill accordingly and the Bill was duly passed by the Meghalaya legislative Assembly as the Meghalaya Succession to Self-Acquired property (Khasi and Jaintia Special Provision) Act 1984, which received the assent of the President of India in 1986. The above act does not apply to the ancestral properties. But the Act of 1986 still lies in the cold storage as the Government failed to formally notify it to give effects to its application. In the year 1990 a new organization named *Syngkhong Rympei Thymmai* was formed with more or less the same objective of the earlier organisation and replaced the other one.

The rules of inheritance of Khasis have an advantage. They prevent the subdivision and fragmentation of land holdings. One of the main reasons for low agricultural productivity in the state of Kerala was reported to be the subdivision and fragmentation of landed property after the disintegration of joint families and the implementation of land reforms in the State, enforcing ceiling on land holdings. The Khasi rule of inheritance checks the fragmentation of landed property but it creates economic disparities even among the members of the same family.

In the matter of succession to authority roles, the whole edifice of inheritance pattern reverts. The eldest brother of the *ka khadduh* succeeded to the authority role of maternal uncle. In the case of succession to Syimship, has another pattern of succession, in which the next uterine brother or in his absence the eldest son of the eldest sister succeeds him. As far as the position of *Syiem Sad* (the high priestess) is concerned the eldest daughter succeeded her mother.

Matriliny: Reactions of Youth

Around two hundred people belonging to all walks of life were interviewed by random and only 22% of them reacted positively to the question whether matriliny is to be changed? 78% of them were of the view that matriliny is an essential part of their culture and their community identity and hence need not be changed. But they felt that changes are required adequate to the needs of the modern world in many aspects associated with matriliny especially in the matters of rules regarding inheritance of self-earned and ancestral property. Other children should not be neglected in favour of the youngest daughter.

A cross section of the youth (males) was also interviewed and asked the question: what are the demerits of matriliny as experienced by them? A major percentage of them believed that it caused economic imbalances in the society and affected the entrepreneurship of the males. Some of the other reactions of the respondents were: it causes identity problems, side-lines males, becoming irresponsible, mismanagement of property, obstruct personality development, etc.

Conclusion

Rapid changes are taking place in many aspects of the organisational set up of the community. It is more visible in towns and villages situated near the urban areas. Among the two studied villages, Nongkrem is in a rural setting and Sawmer, on the other hand, is located in semi-urban surroundings and hence changes are more visible in that village. More and more families have begun to follow patrilocal pattern of residence out of choice or compulsions and in many cases even the male children are getting a share of landed property of their parents. In the case of daughterless parents they are even giving their ancestral property to their male children by some means. Descent is still reckoned on the mother's line but their instinct to recognise also with their father's group can be found in the recent trend of adopting double titles, i.e. of both the parents or at least in suffixing the father's personal name with their own. Contrary to the common practice of registering their land documents in the name of wife, if they purchased a plot of land, more and more of land registrations are now taking place in the name of the male head of the family. Though no drastic changes have taken place in the structural organisation of the community, changes are visible in its functions.

*****

A Khasi boy Carrying the Jackfruit

Khasi Men at Work

Smoking Pipe

A Khasi man with his child

A Khasi Woman in the field

Khasi Women

Khasi women selling Ornaments

Chapter - IV

Khasi and Nair Matriliny: A Comparison

Kerala is a narrow strip of coastal land lying between South Karnataka and Kanyakumari in southwest India. It is bounded by the Western Ghats on the east and the Arabian Sea on the west. It has the distinction as the most literate state in the Indian Union. The land of Kerala before the formation of a modern state was part of different regional kingdoms. There were three political divisions- Travancore, Cochin and Malabar. Travancore and Cochin were separate princely states and Malabar was a province under erstwhile Madras presidency. A unique system of social stratification based on caste system was prevalent in Kerala. The caste-ranking practice was more elaborate and even sub-castes were hierarchically ordered. In this hierarchy, the Namboodiri Brahmins occupied the top most position, depended much on its ritual purity, wealth and political power. Various Kshatriya castes who were fewer in number came next to Brahmins. They were the rulers and owned vast stretches of land. Some of the royal matrilineages, though of Nair origin, claimed the status of Kshatriya, the second in the Varna category of the Hindu system. These matrilineages as the royal families claimed superiority over others.

Below the Namboodiris there were a few temple-serving castes, like Ambalavasis, Marars, Varriers, etc., but were numerically small. The Nairs occupied a position just below them and they owned landed properties. The Tiyas/Iravas come next in the caste hierarchy.They were mainly toddy-tapers from the coconut and palm trees. They held land on sub-tenure from Nambudiri landlords and Nair tenants. The astrologer community of Kanisans and the artisan communities like Kollan (blacksmith), Tattan

(Goldsmith), Aasaris (carpenters), Kallasaris (stonemasons) occupied more or less a similar status in the local caste hierarchy. The communities like Velinchans (Barbers) and Mannans (Washer men) were also part of the system but the communities with higher caste status like Nairs received their services only on specialised occasions like death, menstruation, childbirth, etc. On other occasions, they had their own community barbers (Vilakkithala Nairs) and washerman (Veluthedan Nairs), and they were sub-castes of Nairs, but occupy a lower position. All these above-mentioned communities were polluting to the Nairs and Brahmins but not as polluting as the Pulayas and the Parayars. The Pulayas were the tillers of soil and they worked in the land of Nambudiris, Nairs, and the Tiyas. The Parayas were the basket and umbrella makers (Schneider and Gough: 1961).

The Nair/Nayar

In this report for the sake of comparison between matrilineal systems of Nairs and Khasis, the matrilineal systems of Nairs, as it existed in the past, have been referred (as available in the literature), and hence whenever referred to the matreilineal systems of Nairs, past tense is used. Because the Nair matriliny in its traditional form does not exist anywhere in Kerala as the Nair society had gradually given up the matrilineal system and adopted the nuclear family mode and equigeniture rule of inheritance patterns though they still reckon their descent matrilineally. The matrilineal system in Kerala is referred to as *marumakkathayam: marumakkal* meaning nephews and nieces and *thayam* means 'line' or 'way'. The inheritance was through nieces and the succession of authority through nephews. It signified that the relationship between a man and his sisters' children was crucial.

According to the 1901 census, there were 116 sub-divisions among the Nair in the erstwhile Travancore state; similar variety of sub-divisions was found in the erstwhile Cochin and Malabar areas also. The nomenclature in the three political divisions also showed considerable variation. The Nairs belong to the Hindu fold and are part of caste society. In the local caste hierarchy, though the Nairs fall in the category of Sudras in the Varna system, they came next to the Nambudiri Brahmins in caste heirarchy. The Brahmins were the ritual leaders and the carriers of the Sanskrit language and of ancient Vedic culture. Descent among the Nambudiris was patrilineal except among a small component of Brahmin community residing in the Payyanur Taluk of Kannur District, which followed the matrilineal system of descent. The Brahmins were also the landlords. Marriage (*sambandam*) between Nambudiri men and Nair women was in practise (hypergamy), however hypogamy was not allowed.

The Joint Family

The joint matrilineal family (*taravad)* was a diagnostic feature of the Nair. A *taravad* might have had thirty or forty members living in the same house and eating from the same kitchen. It traced descent from a common ancestress, through several matrilineages (*tai vazhi* –tai means mother and vazhi means line or way in Malayalam). Every member, male and female, had an equal right to the property, but that could be transmitted only through the female members. The eldest male member of all the combined matrilineages was the *karanavar*, who had the right to manage the properties, as a trust, on behalf of all the members. Over the centuries, it became an absolute power, which, however, most *karanavans* exercised only after informal consultations with his senior female relatives. Residence after marriage was mostly matrilocal for the women and avunculocal for the men, but the *karanavan* could bring the wife to live with him; she then became the *ammayi*, a figure feared and loved by the female members of the family. She had roles to perform during life cycle rituals of the girls of the family. However, she had no right to the property of her husband's family; when he died; she had to leave his family, taking nothing but her personal belongings with her, before his body could be removed to cremation ground. In the Malabar area of Kerala there was a slight difference in the residence pattern where after marriage the couple stayed with the husband's matrilineal group but once the husband was dead she had to go back to her matrilineal group and she and her children had no right over his property. The children would join their mother's matrilineal joint family when they were five or six years of old. The members of the same *taravad* observed *pula* (pollution attached to birth and death of relatives) on occasions like birth and death. Matriliny in Kerala was humane. Though the system was not matriarchal – women did not govern the household- it accorded them greater freedom, choice and respect than they would have found elsewhere in the world until the twentieth century (Saradamony, 1991).

If a joint family became too large, it found practical solutions. Land in those days was still readily available, and a family could simply agree to divide itself: one branch would take up land elsewhere. Matrilineal joint families appear to have partitioned themselves in this way whenever it made sense to do so. In the 1920's *karanavans* tyranny and highhandedness were said to drive young Nairs to leave home, where life was often worse than under slavery. Between the 1920's and the 1950's, disarray and disputes in matrilineal families affected the lives of hundreds of thousands of people in Malabar, Cochin and Travancore. Intense and widespread, the problem drove people to try to change laws relating to inheritance and marriage. The turmoil in the family led to fights, murders and court cases (Saradamony, 1991).

Talikettu Kalyanam and Sambandham

Two distinct ceremonies marked a girl's progress towards sexual unions among the Nairs. The first was *talikettukalyanam*- the tali (marriage badge) tying marriage. A Brahmin tied a *tali,* a small ornament around the necks of a number of young girls prior to their first menstruation. It was not necessary that it should be done by a Brahmin but can be done by a *mura checkan* (mother's brother's son). The man who tied the *tali* rarely became the sexual partner of the any of the girls. But in the case of *muracheckan* he could later marry her if the family wished so.

Sambandham is real marriage. A *sambandham* partner of a woman only visited her at night; they did not live with her in her *taravad.* Both women and men were permitted several s*ambandham* partners and relationship could be broken by either party at will. A woman's children belonged to her own *taravad.* They have no right in the property of their father. The system continued till the end of the eighteenth century and it began to change by the beginning of the nineteenth century.

The children of *sambandham* union were the responsibility of his/her mother's family where they grew up among their mother's relatives. Children, even if their fathers happened to be Brahmins or Kshatriyas, often had little to do with their fathers. In North Malabar though matriliny prevailed, women usually went to their *sambandham* partners' house during his lifetime, and returned to their own after his death. This contrasted with the custom elsewhere of the remaining in their own house. Yet in spite of the variations, the broad outline holds true (Fuller, 1976).

One another factor that contributed to the practise of *sambandham* was the Nambudiri custom that only the eldest member of the family should marry with in their caste, and the junior members should find their spouses in the Kshatriya and Nair castes without being subject to the obligation of providing for their sustenance and other worldly needs (Saradomony, 1991).

Deprivation of Soldering

The earliest Portuguese accounts described the Nairs as the members of militia, distinguished for their fighting skills. They were warriors under different regional kingdoms. Once the British disarmed the Nairs through out Kerala in the 1810's, the matrilineal joint family was forced to cope with peace, a condition it had seldom known before. Peace deprived young Nairs of soldiering, hitherto their most important occupation and led to an increased population.

Marthanda Varma of Travancore was the first to successfully break from the tradition of solely depending on the Nair fighters. He engaged mercenaries, trained in the European manner by De Lannoy. The brilliant success of his army over the rest of Kerala has to be credited to the imposition of discipline of drilled operations, against the confused and dispersed exhibition of individual martial virtuosity, which had been the hallmark of Nair techniques. The cavalry of the Mysore Sultan has completely discomfited the Nair; the artillery and the tactical drill of the British army completed the process. The old kalari skills (a martial art) became obsolete as tactical methods (Menon, 2002: 799).

"The cessation of the fighting role of the Nair as a community led to the return of the males from a peripatetic to a settled life, in the bosom of their taravads"(ibid). Deprivation of soldering led to increasing unemployment, growth of population, pressure on land, etc. As the problem became intense and widespread, it drove the people to try to change laws relating to inheritance and marriage.

The Disintegration of Matrilineal System

Its degeneration set in only when, under the impact of western civilization, the tendencies of the educated section began to draw them to the universal system of patriarchy. The educated section of the community began to agitate for legislation to validate the *sambandham* form of marriage.

Nayar Service Society (NSS)

The movement towards patriliny was sponsored by the Nair Service Society; the caste organization covering all sub-groups which revolted against *marumakkathayam* (matrilineal) system of inheritance. Its leaders (like Mannath Padmanabhan) advocated family reform. They argued for legal recognition of patriliny so that a man's property would be descended to his wife and children, not his nephews and nieces. They also demanded that any member of the matrilineal joint family be given the legal right to claim his or her shares of the family's asset. The prior traditions that it had been divisible only with the unanimous consent of all adult members need to be lifted. Mannam also tried to abolish the sub group distinctions among them to weld them in to a united community (Saradamony, 1991).

Legislations and Decline of Matriliny

Legislative attempts to reform matriliny began in the 1890's and extended in to the 1970's. The Madras Government's Malabar Marriage Act of 1896 first allowed Nairs to register a *sambandham* as a marriage. This allowed a man to bequeath his self-acquired property – but not his share in the matrilineal joint family – to his wife and children. Previously, his own property passed automatically to the collective property holding of his joint family. In the first two years of the Act, only 51 marriages were registered and by 1906 it was pronounced a dead letter with only one or two marriages a year being registered (Iyer, 1995).

A law was enacted in Travancore (south Kerala) in 1912 regulating marriage, succession, and family management of the Nairs. It legalised *sambandham* as valid marriage, and made it obligatory on the part of the husband to maintain his wife and minor children. It altered the customary law of inheritance by conferring the right of inheritance on a Nair man's property (self-acquired) on his wife and children. This paved the way for the complete overhauling of the social organisation of the community. The fact that about 34,000 *taravads* (matrilineal joint family) partitioned their properties with in five years of the passing of the regulation is proof of the eagerness of the community to avail itself of the permissive legislation. The obligation thrown on the husband or father to maintain the wife/children, combined with the right of the wife and children to acquire the self-acquired property of the husband/father made hypergamous marriages (the marriage between Nair women and Namboodiri men) very rare. The restrictions made on the dissolution of marriage made divorce less frequent. The regulation had rung the death knell of matriliny. The Cochin Nair regulation was passed in 1920 to regulate and amend the law of marriage, inheritance, succession, family management and adoption on the same lines as in Travancore. In 1933, the Madras Marumakkathayam Act was passed to change the structure of family organization and the mode of inheritance in Malabar (Iyer, 1995).

The Travancore Nair Act 1925 offers right to individuals to demand division of family and per capita sharing of assets. Wife and children were entitled to all self acquired property of a man. The Cochin Nair Act 1938 also was in similar line, which enabled individuals to demand per capita division of family assets. There were also a few other legislations as well such as Madras Maumakkathayam (Amendment) Act 1947, Cochin Maumakkathayam (Amendment) Act 1948, Hindu Succession Act 1956, Maumakkathayam (Amendment) Act 1958, etc., passed at time to time by the princely states of Travancore and Cochin, Madras Presidency under

British rule and after independence the state of Kerala as well as the Union Government. All these Acts ultimately helped in shaking many of the customs and practises of Nairs which stood as supporting pillars of their matriliny (Saradamony, 1991).

In 1976, however, the Government of Kerala swept away the most substantial vestige of matrilineal joint family system. The Joint Hindu Family System (Abolition) Act withdrew recognition of the "corporateness" of such families: thereafter, the law deemed them to have been partitioned, and as members died their shares no longer were simply absorbed back into the family, but were inherited by their children or other legal heirs. Economic surveys demonstrated that Nairs were losing land. In Travancore between 1920 and 1929, they were found to have had a net loss of property worth Rs. 8 million. In the same period, Christians experienced a net gain of property worth Rs.4.7 million. Mostly legislations enacted during pre-British, British and post independence period led to the collapse of matrilineal system in Kerala (Saradamony, 1991).

Nair and Khasi Matriliny: A Comparison

Though both the Khasi and the Nair communities fall in the wider category of matrilineal societies they differ widely in its structure, function and components. Still a few parallels are observable. Differences are more than similarities. The following table shows the major differences in the basic components of matrilineal systems between Khasis and Nairs.

Table 11: Differences in the Basic Components of Matrilineal Systems of Khasis and Nairs

	Khasis	*Nairs*
1.	Residence after marriage is Matrilocal or Neolocal.	Residence after marriage was Avunculocal or Duolocal (Now being Patrilocal or Neolocal).
2.	After the death of a wife, or divorce a man returns to his mother's residence (*iing*).	After the death of one's husband or divorced wife returns to her matrilineal joint family (*taravad*)(In Malabar area where residence was avanculocal on the boy's side.)
3.	Children of a couple continue to stay with their maternal grandparents if their parents separate and mother died or remarries.	Children used to return to their mother's *taravad* after attaining the age of five or six even if their parents are living in the father's house.
4.	Cross-cousin marriages of first degree though not prohibited is not practised.	Cross-cousin marriages preferred.

(*Contd...*)

5.	Marriage by exchange is considered to be a sin.	Marriage by exchange is a very common type of marriage.
6.	Inheritance is unigeniture, I,e, the family property goes to the youngest daughter.	The *taravad* property goes to all irrespective of sex or age (equigeniture) but strictly on matrilineal line.(*Talla Vazhi*- *Talla* means mother and *Vazhi* means line i.e, following mother's line).
7.	*Iing* property is not a corporate unit.	*Taravad* property is a corporate unit.
8.	A man after marriage lives in wife's house and works on her land.	A man continued to stay in his house and worked in his *taravad* property.
9.	The Khasi families are mostly nuclear or in the case of a *khadduh* it is an extended family with wife's parents and unmarried siblings.	The Nair family is a joint family, extended both vertically and horizontally.
10.	The maternal uncle is the head of the family, but he resides in a different house (in his wife's residence)	Maternal uncle was the head of the family and he resides with his maternal family members. He can bring his wife to his residence.
11.	Khasis follow monogamy.	The Nairs were serial monogamous or fraternally polyandrous.
12.	There are no hypergamous marriages	Hypergamous marriages were present. The Nair women engaged in marital relations (*sambandham*) with Namboodiri men but not vice versa.

The 'matrilineal puzzle' (the term coined by Andrey Richards) i.e., the tension which is bound to arise between the husband and the matrilineal descent group into which he is married, more specifically over the question of control over the wife and children is visible among most of the matrilineal communities. In several communities, they have their own inherent structural mechanisms to deal such puzzles. Among the Nairs, this was solved to some extend by the institution of preference of cross-cousin marriages and the institution of avanculocal (residence after marriage with boy's uncle) residential patterns. Since the wife's father is one's own mother's brother, the scope for tension between the two was very negligible. In the case of Nairs, the residence pattern was avanculocal, i.e. the couple after marriage stayed with the matrilineal relatives of the husband and hence no question of tension between the husband and his wife's matrilineal relatives over the question of authority over the wife and children.

But in the case of Khasis the situation is different. The type of structural arrangements available among the Nairs are non- existent among them. The cross-cousin marriages are prohibited and the residence after marriage is matrilocal. In such a situation, the condition of males after marriage will be miserable and is one of tension and conflict. The condition is more so in case of those who marry a heiress because she is to be more loyal to her matrilineal kin group than to her husband. In case of non-heiress once they establish their own households, the husband will have more say over his wife and children than a husband of heiress. But even in that case whatever they earn will go to his wife and children and if he buys a little bit of property that would be registered in their wives' names and not in their own.

Among the Nairs, though matrilineal, the condition of wives especially those who married non-cross cousins was miserable as she had to go and stay with her husband's matrilineal relatives. There she has to face several adjustmental problems. There was a saying *ammayiamma poru* that is the fight between mother-in-law and daughter-in-law. And in that house the wife has to suffer several discriminations and she is always considered as secondary to the own daughters of the mother. The sort of puzzle and tension suffered by the Nair wives in their husbands' residence is possible to be suffered by the Khasi males in their society. After marriage they have to go and stay with their wives' relatives and there their personality is seldom honoured; in fact they were considered as secondary citizens. More than that where he is going and living with are aliens till the other day and they have to make a lot of adjustments there. Since the system of cross-cousin marriage is not there the in-laws are totally new to them.

In case of Nairs after the death of a husband, the wife and children leave her husband's residence and join her matrilineal family in which she and her children have a right of ownership. Her presence there was not objected by anybody since they have a legal right of ownership there since the *taravad* property is a corporate one. But in case of Khasis it is the man who has to return to his natal home after the death of his wife. He also has to leave the children under the custody of their matrilineal relatives that in this case is the *khadduh* of the family. Normally he can come and stay with his mother if she is alive or with his *khadduh* sister, who was normally accepted him happily. But since the property of the *iing* is not corporate that type of rights and privileges, which the Nair girls enjoyed at her residence, is not available to a widowed Khasi man in his natal home.

Marriage by exchange is a common type of marriage among the Nairs. Since the sisters are exchanging to each other it struck a balance in many aspects of the life. It is expected that since one's own daughter is living with the family of her in laws she will give more considerations to her daughter-in-law since every action will have an equal reactions on her own daughter living with her in-laws relatives.

Since the Nair karanavan is a co-resident of the joint family he could properly manage the *taravad* property and bring discipline in the family. His presence is always there and the family members respect him with revere and deviation from the family norms was put down by him. At the same time he can be closer to his wife and children because the residence is avanculocal. But as far as the Khasis are concerned the residence pattern is an obstruction for such proximities with his maternal relatives.

The *kpoh* organization of Khasi is similar to the taravad of the Nairs in its composition but it differs drastically in its function. The *kpoh* does not have a head but the Nair *taravad* was under the authority of a Karanavar. The Nair *taravad* was also a corporate unit owning landed properties in common and the income from the property is used for the living of its members. It is also a dwelling unit, though the female members shift temporarily to their husbands' residence after marriage. It, at the same time, accommodates the wife and the younger children of the male members even though they are not the members of a *taravad.* When the *taravad* property divides all its members would get a share but the wife and children of the male members though co-residents of the joint family omitted and the female members and their children though not a resident at that point of time would be included. The *karanavan* though he is the titular head of the family and manager of the property cannot inherit a share of the property to his children. When the dwelling unit become so big to accommodate all its members the taravad may split up on the direct line of their sisters of the karanavar. If he has three sisters they may divide in to three lines and the property is divided according to the total number of the members in each line. Disputes between nephews and nieces on one side and children of a man on the other for property were common in Nair families because the *taravad* was a property group but it is very rare in Khasi society.

The Nair community was part of a unique system of social stratification based on caste system prevalent in Kerala. The caste-ranking practise was more elaborate and even sub-castes were hierarchically ordered. Such social stratification based on caste system was not present in Khasi society, and hence no superior or inferior divisions among them and hence no hypergamous marriages. The Nair women used to engaged in such marriages with Namboodiri men who were in the upper strata of caste hierarchy.

Out Migration

It is generally believed that the lack of stake in the family property and the feeling of isolation at home are the two reasons by the males in the matrilineal societies to migrate with in and outside the region and the country. It is generally believed that it is an outlet to their frustration. Minangkabau are one of the 300 ethnic communities in Indonesia. Their population is estimated at 3.4 million according to 1980 census (cited in Govindan Unni 1994: 4). Modern sociologists are referring to the Minangkabau as the world's largest matrilineal society - of course after the disintegration of matrilineal system among the Nairs of Kerala (cf. Hans-Dieter Evers 1974). Various accounts show over a million Minangkabau of Sumatra islands living outside (Govindan Unni 1994:33). Out migration is considered an essential feature of the Minangkabau matrilineal custom; go abroad and make good has been the motto. A youth who fails to do so could be looked down upon as a failure in society. Keralites too migrates in a large scale essentially for economic reasons. Their migration accelerated after the Second World War. They can be seen in sizable groups in the Gulf countries, the United States, Canada, Malaysia and Singapore. A study estimates the total number of Keralites outside the state in 1982 at 1.8 million (Gopinathan Nair, 1983:4).

But in the case of Khasis the picture is different. The Khasi boys generally do not prefer to go outside the state for education or for seeking employment. During the present study it was found several people resigning their jobs or taking long leaves to avoid transfers to other places even to Guwahati or even to the Ri Bhoi district of the same state. Though the North East and particularly Shillong have several defence organizations the number of Khasis working in these organizations is too scanty. Generally they dislike such jobs, which require long time absence from their kith and kin. Many of the informants told that their recruitment in to the police force began only recently and earlier they hesitated to join even such forces alike.

Conclusion

The matrilineal system among Nairs began to disintegrate by the middle of the Nineteenth century and the process was more or less complete by the second half of the twentieth century. Its decline was not due to a single factor but was a cumulative outcome of wide variety of factors operated in that society. Western education, growth of population, introduction of commercial crops and cash economy were a few of them. The traditional structure of the society collapsed and the results were complex. The most important advantage was the reform of family law, recognition of Nair liaisons as effective marriages and the legalisation of the partition of the joint family properties, and therefore of individual inheritance and alienability (Renjini 2000:14). The collapse of the traditional structure facilitated the growth of socialist and communist movements and the first Communist ministry initiated the "Family Planning Programme" to check increasing population pressure. The attitudes of the Nairs towards the family have changed dramatically. Today the model family of mother, father and one or two children has become increasingly widely shared with patrilocal or neolocal pattern of residence and equigeniture mode of inheritance. But the Khasi society still follows the matrilineal system as steadfastly as possible but elements and forces of changes are already visible in the Khasi matrilineal system. The first major onslaught came from Christianity as the Khasi matriliny is woven around and developed surrounding the religious premises of the community. Still the Khasis could accommodate Christian faith without many changes in their culture and following other aspects of their culture like kinship, family, residence, inheritance pattern, marriage rules, etc., intact. It is this accommodative nature of the Khasi community which helped them to continue with their tradition while accepting the elements of modernity. While many of the legislations among the Nairs helped to disintegrate Nair matriliny, among the Khasis some of the laws passed by the Khasi Hills Autonomous District Councils helped to strengthen their traditional systems. More than that, the wind of changes sown by the pro-changers of matrilineal systems in the Khasi society could not create that type of an impact which the pro-changers among the Nairs could achieve. As a result of these the Khasi matriliny continues to follow unabated in spite of the fact that the factors of changes are clearly visible in that society.

*****

A War Khasi Man returning home from the field

A War Khasi Man

A War Khasi Woman

The Traditional way of Carrying the child

Modern Khasi houses

Chapter - V

Structural Alignment of Male and Female Roles in Khasi society

It is generally believed that the position of women in matrilineal societies is more comfortable than in patrilineal societies. But no matrilineal society, at least in India, can be found where the women enjoyed absolute authority and power. The Khasi society is not an exception. In this context it is important to analyse the structural alignment of the role, power and function of both men and women in Khasi society. The position of both men and women was traditionally ascriptive rather than achieved. Based on customary beliefs and practices, the male vis-a-vis female roles were structurally defined. The man is the protector and provider whereas the women is the procreator as well as perpetuator and the sustaining root of kinship and traditions. What has been investigated is whether the traditionally defined and structurally implicated role performance of the male is affecting the achievement of males in the context of present day realities and is it causing any stress and strain on the male members of the community.

Women's Position in the Society

The Khasi society is still governed by tradition under a unique system of matrilineal society. Even after the three decades of statehood either the Meghalaya Government or Autonomous District Councils in the state have not enacted any specific legislation to regulate or streamline the social behaviour relating to family affairs. In the absence of such a law the Khasi community was under the traditional customs and usages in relation to inheritance and descent.

As far as the principle of descent is concerned it is reckoned through the female line. The affiliation of a member to a group is determined by his or her birth and it cannot change under any circumstances. It is important for a woman that her children (whether male or female) carry her title and not of her husband. The continuity of the family is through its female members and hence the parents prefer a female child to ensure the continuity of its lineage.

The inheritance of ancestral property is also on the female line. But the underlying principle of female ultimogeniture rule of inheritance (i.e. inheritance through the youngest daughter) is the negation of the rights of other daughters, except the youngest, over the property of their parents. This is one of the areas of stress and strain felt even by the female members of the community. Even though the youngest daughter was only the custodian of the ancestral property in the past, the situation has changed a lot by now and at present she is more or less considered as the legal heiress. As the community has advanced from subsistence based economy to an economically stratified society, the system of inheritance is creating imbalances as far as the economy of the other members of the family is concerned. It was observed that while the youngest sister was living in posh houses enjoying a lot of economic liberties, her own siblings trying hard to make a living.

The residence after marriage is matrilocal or neolocal as the case may be. Here also the elder sisters are deprived in favour of the youngest one. If the parents are rich enough to part a plot of land for their elder daughters they are lucky enough to build a house, otherwise they have to live in rented houses till the husband and wife could pool enough money to build a house of their own. The elder daughters, even after the establishment of their own houses, continue to maintain their relationships with their ancestral home, but they have to establish themselves as the continuity of their *iing* stem from that particular household.

As far as the authority pattern is concerned it is always bestowed on the maternal males. The maternal uncle is the manager of the ancestral property and in his absence the elder brother of the *ka khadduh* manages it. He takes all the important decisions as far as the management of property, religious and social events, etc., are concerned. But there exists a dual authority structure in the household. Matters, especially those pertaining to the children are always the privilege of the father to look after. There is no clear-cut boundary that where the authority of the father ends and where the authority of the maternal uncles begins. It always overlaps and hence it is an area where there is a possibility of conflicts of interests between father and maternal uncle and the female members suffers in between.

In the family the mother reigns supreme in the management of the house. Besides rearing the children and preparing the food the mother is also responsible for the budgeting economy of the family. She pools the income and manages the family. She does even the purchases for the day-to-day affairs and the male members usually do not interfere.

The Khasi women are hardworking and entrepreneurial. They are not a lot keeping indoors looking after only the household chores. They help their men folk in the agricultural fields, businesses and even engaging in their own businesses, both petty and large. Many of them have found employment in the State and Central Government services. They are found to be more enterprising than the men. Even where the husbands become lazy and irresponsible without contributing anything towards the maintenance of the family, the womenfolk will take the sole responsibility of looking after the family affairs and hence they are economically independent. In business, the females outnumber the males, especially in petty trades, like opening of vegetable and fruit stalls, sale of fish, dry fish, trade of lime and betel nuts, running of tea and grocery shops, etc. Though in the initial years the men outnumbered their womenfolk as far as their number in the Government Service was concerned, the women folk are found gradually excelling their counterparts in that area as well. In the Meghalaya Secretariat 64% of the employees are women (Nessa, Saifun, 2005).

Table 12: Female-Male Workers in Meghalaya

	Male	*Female*	*Total*
Main Workers	585,520	336,055	921,575
Cultivators	242,805	167,465	411,270
Agriculture Labourer	70,460	44,182	114,642
Household Industries	6,459	5,510	11,969
Other Workers	264,796	118,898	383,694
Marginal Workers	118,189	145,855	264,044
Non Working	**788,123**	**993,147**	**1,781,270**

Source: Census of India, 2011.

The above table shows that the share of female workers in the state is as close as male and they are contributing equally towards the economy. The proportion of female and male workers in Meghalaya in 2001 was 35 per cent and 47.8 per cent, respectively. According to the Census of 2011, it is 38.45 per cent and 48.30 per cent, respectively. The percentage of female workers has increased and the gap between them and the male workers is narrowing indicating that the female contribution to the economy is more or less equal to the male contribution. According to a survey of 2001-2002 the Rural Work Force Participation Rate (WFPR) was much higher in Meghalaya than the National average. The WFPR in Meghalaya was stated to be 418 as against a National average of 299, while that of urban areas was 197 vis-à-vis the all India figure of 139.

Social issues such as dowry deaths and harassment at the hands of in-laws are unknown among the Khasis. Not only in patrilineal societies but also in matrilineal societies, which follow the patrilocal pattern of residence, the possibilities of harassment or disagreement between mothers-in-law and daughters-in law were quite possible. Even among the Nairs, an erstwhile matrilineal community of Kerala, the females who come in to the joint family of their husbands after marriage had to suffer harassment from the maternal female relatives of their husbands. In the household she had to observe several restrictions which were not practically applicable to the in-born female members of the t*aravad* (joint family).

The males enjoy exclusive political, judicial and religious powers and women are deprived of all these. The women cannot participate in clan or village *dorbars* wherein the membership is exclusively limited for the adult male members though very recently some of the local dorbars have included the women of the locality as well as in the Electoral College to elect the headman but their involvement in the totality of its functioning is quite limited. The *Syiem* is the political head of the Khasi State. But his children cannot succeed him to the post after his death. It is the eldest sister's eldest son who succeeds his maternal uncle. Though the *Syiem* is the Chief of the State, his mother or the eldest sister is the head and custodian (*Syiem Sad*) of religion. Thus even though the political power is vested on the male members it is succeeded only through the female line. The representations of women in the State Assembly as well as in the District Councils are also very negligible. But in the matter of economy it reverts the whole edifice of power structure.

There is no doubt that women in the Khasi society are enjoying more power, both socially and economically. But even among the female folk, the norms and values of the community are bringing disparity as far as the enjoyment of economic resources is concerned. It also does not mean that the position of women in Khasi society is absolutely tension-free. In many cases, the husbands are found to be turned irresponsible, being addicted to drink and in such cases the women has to take the sole responsibility of the family. Their economic self-dependency helps them in such situations to withstand such onslaughts in their life. The health statuses of the Khasi women are also found deteriorated due to frequent deliveries and hard labour.

The infant mortality rate (IMR) is the single most important indicator, illustrating the level of human development of a nation or state. An IMR below ten indicates a high level of development and in India , Kerala with an IMR of 14, is the only state that is approaching this level. According to the Sample Registration System Bullettin the IMR in Meghalaya is 58.

According to Indian Nutrition Profile, Meghalaya has 67.6 per cent of anemia children between 6 and 35 months. According to the Union Ministry of Labour, Meghalaya have 34,633 child labour forces next only to Assam in the North East Region (Joshi, 2005).

The sex ratio in the state improved from 958 females against 1000 males during 1991 to 975 in 2001 and to 1013 in 2011. The number of female-headed households was appreciably high in state with 23.6% in rural pockets and 28.9% in urban areas. Female literacy rate increased from 45% during 1991 to 60% during 2001 and to 78.50 per cent in 2011. The Census of India 2011 proves that in most of the C.D.Blocks in East Khasi hills and Jaintia hills districts female literacy rates are higher than the male literacy rates.

Families are essential institutions which have a vital role not only in the socialization process but also in conducting the behavioural activities relating to the wide range of life, needs specific guidelines. As far as marriage is concerned, a majority of people are still governed by tradition with the exception of Christian communities which is governed by the Christian Marriage Act. A few prerogative class and in cases of inter-caste marriages take the protection of civil marriages in the court. Other than these, they are still in a confusing state, thus separation and broken homes multiply as days rolled on resulting in multiplication of uncared children. Traditionally the fathers have nothing to do with their children once the parents separated and it was the mother and her clan that take care of their upkeep and other responsibilities. (Lyngdoh, 2005).

The data from the field proves harassment of women is not a matter of rare occurrence. Husbands beating wives are not infrequent in Khasi society. But such cases are more in nuclear than in matrilineal extended families. In the matrilineal extended families, the presence of close relatives of the wives often restricts the husbands from resorting to atrocities against wives and children. In nuclear families, the situation is different and the husband enjoys more freedom and power in decision making and thus have increased command over his wife and children. It needs to be explored whether the husband's alcoholism and wife beating and such other activities is actually a mechanism to relax the mental tension caused by the matrilineal familial surroundings.

"Divorce was never considered a taboo in Khasi matriliny. A married couple could mutually agree to leave one another and the children would remain with the mother. Perhaps the only inconvenience was that the mother had to single-handedly bring up the children. But at a time when family ties were strong , needs were relatively simpler, education the luxury of the few and the clan members played an important role in providing financial and emotional support, the stress and strain remained hidden" (Mukhim; 2002b).

About 82% of the respondents believe that incompatibility is the major reason for a high divorce rate in the society. They felt that as long as the in-laws (especially the mother-in-law), do not interfere in the matters of husband and wife, there arises no question of incompatibility and it arises when the in-laws interfere. They had shown, for instance, the high rate of divorces at a later stage of marriage, usually after getting one or two children. If it is the incompatibility between husband and wife, it would have taken place at an earlier stage of marriage. The in-laws interference in family matters even in matters concerning the children creates a sense of 'unimportance' among husbands and it leads to ego clashes and divorce. The in- laws interference is visible in many fields concerning children's education, purchase of family property, savings, etc. Though there is difference in degree, such influences are there even in households where they live neolocally. The husbands feel diminished and self-respect undermined when the wives begin to neglect his view in favour of her relatives. The same section of the respondents also share the view that the areas the matriliny places the male in a position of great disadvantages are in decision making and financial management. The recent trend among those who can afford to is to live away from in-laws to avoid such intervening influences. The increase in number of patrilocal and patri-neolocal (neolocal residence near to husbands' parents)residence is proof of this trend. However, in some if the localities of Shillong town like Nongrim Hills, Laitumukhra and Lachumiere women have got space in the village councils as elected or nominated members (Jyrwa, 2005:61).

The state since its formation in 1972 has never been headed by a woman Chief Minister. In 1978 and 1983 Meghalaya Assembly were having no woman representative. In 1988, two women, Maysalin War and Miriam D Shira were elected. The woman representation reduced to one in 1993. Only Roshan Warjri was elected. The number increased to three in 1998. In the 2003 Assembly election also only three women candidates won the election. The lone woman MLA in the Meghalaya Assembly in 2008 was Ampareen Lyngdoh. The 2013 Assembly had the largest representation of women with four members. Only three women MLAs have been elected in the New Meghalaya Assembly of 2018.

There were also men taking advantage of working wives neglecting the family to indulge themselves in evil habits like addiction to drinks. This is not the problem only with matrilineal societies but the situation in Khasi society where in the economic resources were mostly owned and managed by the wives, the husbands get undue advantage to avoid the burden of familial responsibilities and to behave irresponsibly. It also leads to breakdown of marital relationships and add to the number of broken families. This very behaviour pattern at home causes the children to lose the respect and reverence to their fathers. The number of broken marriages is on increase in Khasi society. A survey of mere 150 households spreading in two villages showed about sixteen such cases. A few cases of unwed mothers were also reported during the survey. These types of families along with simple male irresponsibility left the young Khasi women stranded forlorn to fend for themselves. Even though there is no such analytical studies that have taken place in Khasi society, psychologists are aware of the after effects of single parenting. The upbringing of the child by a single parent affects the performance of the child in various activities. The children raised by a single parent are more prone to bad habits like dropouts from school, getting in to fight, alcoholism, etc. Meghalaya rates second in the country in terms of the school dropout rate. Nearly 80% school dropout rate between classes-I to class-X in Meghalaya was reported (Shillong Times, 02-02-2005).

A recent National Health and Family Survey (NHFS) revealed that Meghalaya, the homeland of three major matrilineal communities in India, has recorded an alarming 86 percent of wife beating cases. This is against the all India average of 56 percentages. The report says: "it is not always alcoholism but patriarchal bent of mind which prompted them to beat their wives. Women did hardly participate in the decision making process of traditional institutions like *durbars* and in the modern political institutions like District Councils and State Assembly their representation is scanty".

Meghalaya tops the list of per capita consumption of liquor in the country. The Alcohol consumption rate in Meghalaya is on increase. It goes up from 1, 27, 30,404 bottles of Indian mad foreign liquor during 2002-2003 to 1, 72, 07,844 bottles in 2003-2004 (Meghalaya Guardian,19-06-2004). Studies also show that illicit trafficking in Meghalaya is also on increase. According to a study sponsored by the Centre for science, Health and Economy in Shillong in the age group of 15-25 years around 20 per cent of the people use one or the other different types of narcotic substances. Narcotic drugs used include ethical drugs mixing with other drugs or liquor and such types of sedative, mood elevator and various types of psychotropic drugs (Ghosal, 2004).

Reports also show that the incidence of rape cases is also on increase in the state. According to the Chairperson of the State commission for Women, about 135 cases of rapes have been reported between 2002-2004in Meghalaya (The Shillong Times, 11-05-2005). Cases of child trafficking are also on increase in Meghalaya where three matrilineal communities predominantly inhabit. It is reported that more than three hundred girls have gone missing in the state in the year 2004-2005 alone and it is a significant number for a small state with a small population and most of them belong to low income groups (Das, 2005).

In response to a call for submission of a status report on women trafficking in the state by the Supreme Court, Meghalaya Government quoting archaic records maintained that there is no problem of prostitution in the state. This was contradicted by Shakti Vahini, an NGO, which filed an affidavit in the Supreme Court in this respect, maintaining that the problem of teenaged being forced into prostitution is there in every north-eastern state including Meghalaya. But the data from the field do not correspond with this statement. Evidence of prostitution could not be found in any of the villages studied. But the marriage ties in many cases were found loosely knit and there were many instances of second or third time marriages. In most cases women take initiatives to part with their husbands and incompatibility and irresponsible attitudes were stated as main reason. Women have no problem in getting remarried but in many cases they are found taking the responsibility of rearing the children solely avoiding remarriage. The spread of Christianity has put some break for this trend of frequent divorces and remarriages. This is one of the main contents of the morale preaching of the Christian Churches especially the Catholic denomination and may have an impact in the long run.

The women in Khasi society were forerunners of many innovations. Today a considerable part of the Khasis embraced Christianity and it brought considerable changes in the socio-religious and economic life of the Khasis. It was a woman, Ka Nabon, who showed great courage to convert herself first to Christianity in spite of the stiff resistance from the community. In the sphere of education also, especially in the case of higher education, the female excel males. There are many among them who reached in the highest realm of civil services. The first Khasi graduate was a girl from the Calcutta University (Mathur. 1979:17). Two women from the community have been honoured by the Centre Government by giving Padmashree awards. The Government of India Act 1935 gave limited franchise to women. In 1937 it created space for two women to contest from the reserved constituency of Shillong and in the contest, Ms. Mavis Dunn Lyngdoh, a Khasi woman, won the election. She became the first woman in the Assam Legislative assembly and was the first lady to become a Minister from the North East. Chairmanship of the UPSC, the highest recruiting agency of civil servants of the Union Government and membership of the UGC went to the Khasi ladies at different points of time. They also could ensure their presence in Indian Administrative and Foreign Services besides having several doctors, engineers, Air Hostess, etc., among them.

Grinding poverty and rising unemployment are steadily pulling women down from their earlier elevated positions. The Constitution of India empowers the tribal councils at various levels to make laws in conformity with the local traditions and customs. Thus in matters relating to marriage, sex relations, kinship, inheritance, settlement of disputes, etc., the influence of customary law is noticed to a great extent. Political power, inheritance and the ownership of immovable property are some of the indicators to decide the status of tribal women. Customary law imposes responsibility on the tribal women as custodian of their tradition and culture. There is no space for women in the decision making bodies.

A research study by an NGO, Impulse Network, proved that nearly seventy per cent of the school drop outs end up as child labourers in the state. The reasons were attributed to poverty, family problems, lack of interest in studying, etc., 24 per cent of them are from rural areas while the remaining are from urban and semi-urban areas. 89 per cent of them indulge in various habits like chewing betel nuts, smoking, sniffing dendrite with many of them consuming alcohol (The Sentinel, 18-10-2004).

Many women's organizations have raised voice for women and for bringing development in their society and to fight against social maladies.

TWWADM (Tribal Women welfare and development Association of Meghalaya), formed in 1979, Synjuk Seng Kynthei (formed in 1947) are a few among them.

Men's Position - Stress and Strain

The matrilineal system as exists among the Khasis has several elements, which are sufficient enough to cause stress and strains on the male members of the community. These stresses and strain can be categorised in the following three forms, which are structural, institutional and behavioural. The structure of the matrilineal system itself is sufficient enough to generate stress on the male folk. Several institutions developed around the system, which instead of releasing the strain, are only accelerating it. In many of the matrilineal societies in India there are built-in institutional arrangements that are capable to soothing the tension, which may be experienced by menfolk in matrilineal systems. On the contrary, a close study of the structural and institutional arrangements of the Khasi system gives a different picture. The behavioural patterns as well, which are supposed to be developed around the structural and institutional arrangements of the Khasi matrilineal system instead of releasing the stress and strain suffered by the menfolk are nurturing them.

Behavioural

The behavioural aspects of the culture of the Khasis, which are leading to stress and strain among male members, operate at different levels. It is observed that generally the parents would not show any attitudinal differences towards the male members in favour of their daughters visibly. In a family the parents always prefer female to male children as because the continuity of the family is always through the female line. This is very much evident in a family where there are no female children and they always pray for a female child otherwise the mother would become a *duh-jait.* Most of the parents agreed that though they receive both the sexes equally the birth of the daughter brings more happiness and joy to the family because it ensures the continuity of the family. It also ensures that the property of the family goes to their own children. This type of behavioural pattern, though at first instance appears harmless, may reinforce a feeling among the boys that they are worthless, unable to contribute anything to the structural continuity of the family. In the day-to-day affairs of the children, especially when they are young, such signs of attitudinal differences may cause psychological damages from an early age.

This very feeling of unimportance develops an inferiority complex among them and it adversely affects their performance in all spheres of their life. Even in education its after-effects are visible affecting the performance rate among the boys. The numbers of girl students appearing for higher studies is many folds higher than the boys. As a result the girls outshine the boys in all domains of life and the boys are more unconfident, irresponsible and unsuccessful as compared to the girls.

There are ample instances in their behaviour pattern of the community which will unconsciously squeeze out the manliness of the male children of the society running down their self-confidence and self-respect and eventually developing a sense of carefree attitude and narrow mindedness to all the needs of decent life. They sacrifice all the ultimate to the immediate. Suppose the parents are leaving the station occasionally for some familial needs they entrust all the familial responsibilities to their youngest daughter even though the grown up male children are there with due instruction that she would look after her elder brothers' needs and activity during their absence, thus reducing their sons status to the position of grown up babies. (Lyngdoh, 2005).

Whatever is earned by a Khasi man before marriage by his effort goes to his mother and adds to the family property. This property is later inherited by his youngest sister and cannot be enjoyed by him or his children. Whatever he earned after marriage would go to his wife and children. If he is buying a plot of land with his hard-earned money, as a matter of fact, is to be registered in his wife's name instead of his own. There is no rule that it should be done like that but the wives often compel their husbands to do so on the pretext that otherwise his youngest sister may make a claim over it in future since it is her brother's property. Suppose a man is getting divorce after this he will be nowhere. He cannot reclaim his property. Whatever he earned before marriage goes to his mother and sister and after marriage to his wife. Under such circumstances he may find it hard to make a living. This sort of a situation may create among the males a feeling of unimportance, nothing to contribute towards a society but be a procreator.

The husbands, especially those who live uxorilocally were not treated equally with other members of the household. This differential treatment was clearly visible when an outsider visited the family and in the pattern of introduction of family members; he might be introduced last or even not. This is evident from the quotation from Chi Nakane (1961: 125) "this family system is clearly reflected in the daily behaviour. When we visited the Khasi household of a youngest daughter, if a man (obviously the husband) came first to greet us , he always said 'please wait, my wife (or mother-in- law) is coming'. And it was the wife who entertained us, offering tea or pan and discussing matters with us, while her husband remained silent in the corner of the room, or in the next room. If her uncle or brother was there, he would be the person who talked to us while his niece or sister served us. In such a case, we were seldom introduced to the husband". Such a behaviour pattern was also experienced by the present researcher during his field study.

Institutional

After marriage, a man has to go and live with his wife's family. If the wife is a *khadduh* the man has to live rest of his life in her family house. He may feel suffocated to live in a house other than his own amongst new faces. He has to adjust a lot to maintain the cordiality of the home atmosphere of his wife. As a man he may not be given much importance and rarely conducted in the functioning of the family, since it is a family affair in which he is not a member. He is only a co-resident of the family. Even in matters pertaining to his own children his in-laws interfere with the decisions he may be interested in taking. This is another area in which the male members feel humiliated. The domineering influence of his parent in-law and brothers-in- law prevent him from ascertaining himself. He may also not get sufficient privacy and freedom to interact with his wife and children as she also has to give equal or more attention to her parents and the family affairs as she is the custodian of the family property and responsible to fulfil all the family requirements satisfactorily. This will add to the persisting psychological pressure on the husband.

Traditionally, among the Khasis, the youngest sister was only custodian of their ancestral property, jewellery and the person responsible for conducting all the religious and ceremonial rituals. The British rule in this area misinterpreted this and she became a legal heiress later. It is found that this rule of female ultimogeniture inheritance has resulted in the declining trend in the enterprising spirit of the male members of the community and it adds stress and strain on its male members. When the society was subsistence based and the landed property was sufficient to cater to all its members this pattern of female ultimogeniture inheritance seems to be harmless, but in the present day situation when the landed property is limited and valuable and the community has advanced to a stratified society based on economic resources, this pattern of inheritance matters a lot. It creates a feeling in their men folk that they are unimportant and it may push them to engage themselves in anti-social activities such as addiction to alcoholic drinks.

The matrilineal system affects the individual aspirations, especially of its male members. The system is an impediment to their entrepreneurship as well. Usually the male members, whether it is sons or nephews cannot succeed any business establishment run by their father or maternal uncle even though they have sufficient skills and efficiency to run it. The youngest daughter would inherit it and her husband since coming from an entirely different familial background may not have the sufficient skill endowment to foster such a flourishing establishment and may hence decline it. It is said that the matrilineal system is responsible for this situation.

If at all a male member is enthusiastic enough to start a business establishment or any self-employment venture, the social situation is not encouraging enough. His mother may not be sympathetic enough to part with her property to help him start a business since the earnings will not go to her *iing* but to his wife's family. If at all he approaches any financial firms he has to pledge the land records, which will always be in his mother's or sister's name and cannot do so also. Under such circumstances the men may feel frustrated and may lose their self-respect.

The pattern of residence and inheritance prevalent among them creates a sense of insecurity among the men. They are always under the shadow of their mother before marriage and under wife after marriage. It impedes the growth of entrepreneurship and motivation of men and creates a sense of frustration in them.

A man cannot identify himself with his wife's and children's group with whom he is living because he is not a member of that descent group. At the same time he feels alienated from his own descent group in which he is a member because his relationship with such groups is only formal in nature. Traditionally the *ka khadduh* was only a custodian of family property but now has been raised to the status of a legal heiress. She may consult her brothers for dealing with the affairs of the *iing* but many feel it only as a formality.

The authority always rests with the male members even in matrilineal societies and it is true in the case of Khasis as well. The social scenario of the present day Khasis has widened a lot owing to various process like spread of education, conversion to Christianity, occupational and spatial mobility, etc., and hence the authority structure of the community has also weakened. In the traditional social set-up the authority of the maternal uncles remained unchallenged because the area of authority to be wielded was narrow and limited. More than that when it was a close-knit society, deviations could be checked through negative sanctions but in the present situation the involvement of fathers in the matters of their children has expanded and the limits of authority between maternal uncles and father is not clearly defined and overlaps. In such a situation a man has to act in dual roles as father and as maternal uncle and which are always of conflicting nature to each other.

The fear of venturing into the unknown is very palpable in the male psyche. According to a sample survey it is found that about a dozen people either resigning or taking long leaves from their lucrative jobs once they got transfer to places outside Meghalaya. The present system in the society is not giving enough opportunities for them to assert themselves. Lack of these opportunities in the socialization process is a handicap for them to venture themselves in to something unknown to them. To quote Mukhim (1999): "the tendency is to cling on to the safety of a mother's shadow. Many young men have given up lucrative jobs outside the state because of the same reason. Indecision is the hallmark of a Khasi male. He leaves decision making to his mother before marriage and to his wife after it. How can then an indecisive husband assume the role of a responsible father? A crisis of identity is bound to arise. The irresponsibility of Khasi male is not his own creation. He has not been trained to be responsible nor allowed to take hard decisions for himself as a young man. And by the time he is ready for the marriage it is too late to start learning responsibility".

It is a known fact that responsibility and financial security empower man to assure the position of authority in family and society. In the above mentioned survey about 53% of the respondents viewed that the present social arena does not provide them with much opportunity to attain financial security and thus to assume responsibilities. At the family circle there is a general tendency to side-line sons and prefer to consult daughters on all important matters concerning the family as the daughters have to look after the family even after the parents' time but the sons are temporary residents who are to shift to their wife's residence after marriage. There is a saying in Khasi language "leit iing briew", meaning "going to someone's house" owing to this practice. To quote Lyngdoh, (2005): 'a Khasi so plainly speaking, that natural force of manliness is unconsciously squeezed out of the male children of the society, running their self-confidence and self-respect and eventually developing the sense of carefree attitude and narrow mindedness to all the need of descent life. They sacrifice all the ultimate for the immediate". Thus matriliny creates a very feeling of inferiority and insecurity in the male from the very beginning and cause for set in frustration and it make them grow irresponsible. Some kinds of stress and strain are evident in that society. Aberrations arise with in the matrilineal system mostly due to the change in value systems and the consciousness of its members on the materialistic side of the system in the changing social scenario. The precarious position of the Khasi men is apparent from the quoting below: "traditionally male persons on separation have nothing to do with their children for their day today subsistence. The entire responsibility to upkeep the children after separation is the duty of their mother and her clan. Till today in most cases when wives predeceased their husbands, those husbands are deprived of their children, not allowing them to keep the children by themselves. Relatives from the wives side usually comes forward and claimed the children including the properties and dwelling house, which is their self-acquired property reducing them to a puppet, which in the true sense, can be termed as naked aggression against men of the community who have no certainty in life but discarded as rags" (Lyngdoh, 2005).

The matrilineal puzzle, (the term coined by the Andrey Richards) i.e., the tension which is bound to arise between the husband and the matrilineal descent group into which he is married, more specifically over the question of control over the wife and children is visible among most of the matrilineal communities. In several communities they have their own inherent structural mechanism to solve such puzzles. Among the Nairs this was solved to a greater extend by the institution of preference of cross cousin marriages and the institution of avanculocal (residence after marriage with boy's uncle) residential patterns. Since the matrilineal descent group of the wife is one's own mother's brother and close relatives the scope for tension between the two is very negligible. More than that in a matrilineal society the association between maternal uncles and the nephews is so close and hence no question of tension between the two. In the case of Nairs the residence pattern is avanculocal i.e. the couple after marriage come and stay with the matrilineal relatives of the husband and hence no question of tension between the husband and his wife's matrilineal relatives over the question of authority over the wife and children.

But in the case of Khasis the situation is entirely different. The type of structural arrangements available among the Nairs is non-existent in that community. The cross cousin marriages are prohibited and the residence after marriage is matrilocal. In such a situation the condition of males in that society after marriage is more miserable and is one of tension and conflict. The condition is more miserable in the case of those who marry an heiress because she is to be more loyal to her matrilineal kin group than to her husband. In the case of non-heiress once they establish their own house hold the husband will have more say over his wife and children than a husband of heiress. But even in that case whatever he earns will go to his wife and children and if he buys a little bit of property that will be registered in his wife's name and not in his own.

Cross cousin marriage was the main diagnostic of matrilineal societies. It was an essential part of Garo social structure and it was the most preferred type of marriage among Nairs. Among the Nairs mother's brother's daughters of marriageable age was a rightful prospective wife. She is usually termed as "*murapennu*" as she is her father's sister's son's prospective wife in future. They were kept a type of joking relationship. This was the case among many other matrilineal communities like Kurichians of Kerala and Arumbukuttam Vellalas of Tamil Nadu. Perhaps the only matrilineal community in India which does not prefer cross cousin marriage is the Khasis. Authors like Richards viewed this pattern of marriage would create a healing effect up on the matrilineal puzzle supposed to exist in matrilineal societies. It also regulates the transfer of property with in the same kinship groups.

Among the Nairs, though matrilineal, the condition of wives especially those who marries non-cross cousins is miserable as she has to go and stay with her husband's matrilineal relatives. There she has to face several adjustment problems. There is a saying *ammayiamma poru* that is the fight between mother in law and daughter in law. And in that house the wife has to suffer several discriminations and she is always considered as secondary to the own daughters of the mother. The sort of puzzle and tension suffered by the Nayar wives in their husbands' residence is possible to be suffered by the Khasi males in their society. After marriage they have to go and stay with their wives' relatives and there their personality is seldom honoured and they are considered only as secondary citizens. More than that where he is going and living with are aliens till the other day and they have to make a lot of adjustments there. Since the system of cross cousin marriages is not there the in laws are totally new to them.

In the case of Nairs after the death of a husband the wife and children leave her husbands residence and join her matrilineal family in which she and her children have a right of ownership. Her presence there was not objected by anybody since they have a legal right of ownership there since the *taravad* property is a corporate one. But in the case of Khasis it is the man who has to return to his natal home after the death of his wife. He also has to leave the children under the custody of their matrilineal relatives that in this case is the *khadduh* of the family. Normally he can come and stay with his mother if she is alive or with his *khadduh* sister, which normally accept happily. But since the property of the *iing* is not a corporate unit that type of rights and privileges, which the Nayar girls enjoy at her residence, is not available to a widowed Khasi man in his natal home.

Marriage by exchange is a common type of marriage among the Nairs. Since the sisters are exchanging to each other it struck a balance in many aspects of the life. It is expected that since one's own daughter is living with the family of her in laws she will give more considerations to her daughter in law since every action will have an equal reactions on her own daughter living with her in-laws.

Since the Nair *karanavan* is a co- resident of the joint family he could properly manage the *tharavad* property and bring discipline in the family. His presence is always there and the family members respect him with revere and deviation from the family norms were put down by him. At the same time he can be near to his wife and children because the residence is avanculocal. But as far as the Khasis are concerned the residence pattern is an obstruction for such proximities with his maternal relatives.

The boys among the Khasis seems to be shyer than girls to come out in the presence of an outsider and interact with them. In many instances they are found hiding behind the door curtains while the girls come out and interact with the visitors. During the field study it is found the male members often avoiding questions and keep consulting their wives to answer for some questions relating to the family. This may be because since he is an in-married male member he may not be aware of many details pertaining to that family.

The status of the *khadduh's* husband (*padduh*) is different from that of his other co-brothers. Others have more freedom in the affairs of their own households while that of the p*adduh's* is restricted by the presence of *iing* members of his wife. Obviously the *khadduh*'s husband experiences more of a stress and strain than his co-brothers. On the other hand the *khadduhs* suffers more of a strain than her husband because of her conflict of loyalties. The pressure may be greater in fact if it comes both from her responsibility to her mother and *iing* on the one hand and to her children's father on the other.

Specific areas of role performances and decision making of maternal uncles and fathers were not clearly defined in the traditional social and familial set up of the Khasis. As the avenues widen, the father is to expand his sphere of family responsibilities as well. The maternal uncle has his added responsibility in his own household as the father of his kids. These dual roles as father of his kids and maternal uncle of his nephews and nieces make him incapable to perform his traditional role as maternal uncle as satisfactorily as the custom demands. Other factors influencing role performance are level of education, economic stability, physical proximity, personal interest and involvement, etc. Modern values conflict with the traditional norms. It is the corporate responsibility however of all the maternal male members of the *iing* to be involved of the main issues that concerns their *iing* members.

The Khasi boys generally do not prefer to go outside the state for education or for seeking employments. During the present study it was found several people resigning their jobs or taking long leaves to avoid transfers to other places even to Guwahati or even to the Ri Bhoi district of the same state. Though the North East and particularly Shillong have several defence organizations the number of Khasis working in these organizations are too scanty. Generally they dislike such jobs, which require long time absence from their kiths and kins. Many of the informants told that their recruitments in to the police force began only recently and earlier they hesitated to join even such forces as well.

The male members of the community in case of separation or an early death of their wives are deprived of their children and even the property which they accumulated with their own income. The customary law does not give him any claim either to the property or the children which will automatically go to the maternal relatives or clan of the mother. Relatives from the wives side usually come forward and claim the children including the properties and dwelling house which is their self-acquired property reducing them to a puppet. This type of behaviour pattern as attested by the customary laws is a naked aggression against the male members of the community who have no certainty in life.

A major section of the respondents felt that though the system is not giving enough leverage and power to the male a complete deliverance from the system is not expecting since it is intertwined with their tradition and since tradition still has its hold in the society. But changes in many aspects are unavoidable, for example in the rule of inheritance. They believed that since the historical background in which the matrilineal system originated and developed were no more in existence in Khasi society the system needs changes adequate to the present situation. The system had more of a religious than economic role to play and since conversion to other faiths had shackled this very religious function of the system and since the society has become more and more materialistic not only due to the processes which are taking place inside the community but also due to the national and global forces for which the community had been exposed since many decades by now.

The Mait Shaphrang Movement, which is basically a movement for positive thinking, has been carrying out an "intellectual terrorism" in Meghalaya during last few years and has been demanding for compulsory registration of marriage, be it in the civil court or the churches. According to it increasing cases of violence in the family and the subsequent increase in the broken families were because of the practise of non-registration of marriages. "Unlike other societies the tribal Khasis, Jaintias and Garos have collectively accepted the practise of cohabitation without any sort of civil or church marriages. A lot of husbands move out of the houses at their whim and fancies" (Aibor Dkhar, 2004). The Mait Shaphrang movement for last few years has also initiated campaigns for the equitable distribution of self-acquired and ancestral properties Act.

Among many matrilineal communities like Nairs of Kerala a series of legislations have been passed by the state legislature before and after independence helped for a change from the matrilineal system. The activities of Nair Service Society (NSS) (an association of Nair pro-changers) also played a vital role in bringing change in the system. Among the Khasis in spite of the activities of Syngkhong Rympei Thymmai (SRT), a growing organization of Khasis campaigning for a complete change over to the patriarchal system could not bring much change. The legislations passed from time to time as well were helping to protect matriliny than disintegrating it contrary to what we found in Nair community. The Khasi Hills Autonomous District (Khasi Social Custom of Lineages) Act 2005 is the latest in the series. Although the Act was passed unanimously in the Khasi Hills Autonomous District Council, the constitutional body created under the Sixth Schedule of the Indian Constitution with a mandate to protect the unique traditions and customs of the particular tribe by enacting laws in this end, dates back in 1997, it took about seven years to receive the approval of the Governor of Meghalaya (Chhakchhuak, 2005).

A Khasi family without a child was considered a "dying clan", a status that is traditionally evolved horror. The above legislation enables a Khasi woman who has no female issue to follow the "rap iing" custom, i.e. to adopt a female child and to continue the clan. She assumes the position of a daughter to take care of the social, economic, and ritual activities including all properties of the family. Thus the male children were not entitled to any of their ancestral property; therefore have no solid identity in their own home. It is believed in an era when matrilineal societies world over are facing cultural extinction, a legislation like this would protect their unique matrilineal system. According to a clause of this Act, members of the community who do not adhere to the provisions of the Act will cease to be a Khasi. A Khasi, whether of pure lineage or of mixed parentage, must follow the matrilineal system by taking his/her clan name from the mother's side. The Act also provides for expulsion from the community if a Khasi individual "adopted the personal laws not compatible with Khasi personal laws or customs". A section of the Christian and Muslim Khasis have adopted personal laws other than that of traditional Khasis. The present Act may upset them.

About thirty years back in 1985 vide notification MGP (law) 6/85-2,500-8-10-85, the Government of Meghalaya through its law department came forward with certain questionnaires which were an indication of government's understanding the social and economic deficiency of those traditional customs and usages prevailing in the Khasi society. It was expected at that point of time that such an initiative would streamline the existing unexpected traditions into expressed law for the interest and healthy growth of Khasis to suit the need and purpose of the growing outlook of the people of the present era. (Lyngdoh, 2005).

Many non-Khasi people married Khasi women with the associated economic benefits in mind. They did business in the latter's name and even bought land. Khasis do not have to pay taxes and no need to get a license to start a business. Men from outside Meghalaya married Khasi women to take advantages of such privileges.

Today the possibility of acquiring a piece of land is limited to a few successful Khasis as land is becoming more and more scarce and costly. The land and the permanent modifications one makes on it in the form of construction of houses and cultivation of permanent crops were inherited by the youngest daughter. So the economic imbalance which today one could observe in Khasi society is not merely the matter of economic organization but also the matter concerned with social structure and organization. The General Secretary of the Syngkhong Rympei Thymmai (SRT) was of the opinion that the Khasi matrilineal system was contributing to the deterioration of Khasi economy. Among the Khasis, the youngest daughter inherits the family's ancestral property. But, now, with the growth of nuclear families, the issue of female inheritance itself is being questioned. This type of economic imbalance was not present among other matrilineal communities, like Nairs and Garos. Among the Nairs where inheritance is equigeniture among daughters and since the property is a corporate unit at any time even the male members can fall back on it for their sustenance but the only thing is that they cannot transfer it to their wives and children. Among the Garos also this much of economic disparity among daughters cannot be observed and the economic condition of each household in a village is more or less similar (Nakane, 1961:105). Among the Arumbukuttam Vellalar also the matrilineal system and the rule of female inheritance is not creating any scope for economic imbalance among the female children of the same parents.

There are families where the sons take the clan name of the father and the daughters take the name of the mother. "We just cannot do away with our matrilineal system, no matter what people say. This system is the key to our entire societal culture and structure. If we changed the matrilineal system to anything else then the whole Khasi society, including our traditional system of governance, would come tumbling down" (Chhakchhuak, 2005).

Recent Trends

No society is static. The Khasi society is not an exception. An alternative value system is gradually emerging giving tremendous pressure to the matrilineal systems. This shift is not because of a single factor but it is a cumulative outcome of a wide variety of factors evident in that society today.

One of the integrating principles of the Khasi society is its value system based on its religious beliefs and practises. The matrilineal system also exists surrounding this value system rooted in religion. As far as the Khasis are concerned, the religion and worship was a matrilineal family affair performed by the matrilineal male usually the *kni* at the *khadduh*'s residence. Though the Khasi as a community has *lyngdoh* as priest, at the family level the eldest male would observe it usually the *kni*. Presently, Christianity offers an alternative organised belief system that has a ptrilineal bias and it conflicts and even contradicts matrilineal beliefs. It is a known fact that in the Christian preaching the father, not the maternal uncle, figures prominently. Among the Christians, though the presence of maternal uncles and maternal males bring honour to the occasion yet it is the father who is preferred. During marriages it is the father who gives the bride away publicly. The maternal uncle does it only in his absence.

The Christian missionaries introduced primary and middle English schools not only in towns and cities but also in rural areas. The Roman Catholics have also specialised in public schools and colleges. The spread of education among the Khasis during the last few decades has surely brought some structural changes. Many of them after getting education could enter the government service, which brought occupational and spatial mobility among them. Most of them who could get in to the government service are found settled in and around the Shillong town. They could also engage in different businesses and non-traditional and non-agricultural jobs and thus becoming part and parcel of the urban affluence. This has also helped in inculcating in them certain western values that is not in conformity with their traditional norms and values. In the little stratified Khasi society, a middle class is gradually emerging based on urban-centered affluence, education and wealth. The urban centered self-sustainability and spatial mobility result in the decreasing influence of the matrilineal groups on its members.

With the introduction of educational institutions and the beginning of large-scale enrolment of students in these institutions they became the meeting place of students from all communities and cultures and as a result of interaction they began to know more about other cultures and people and exchange of culture traits became irresistible.

The role and control of maternal uncles on their sisters and their children is also becoming thin and slacken due to the lack of proximity and presence due to the spatial mobility. The maternal uncle has to give prominence to his own career, entertainment, and his own children to whom they are more attached. When the maternal authority relinquishes the paternal responsibilities and authorities are on increase. The tendency among the youth, especially among those settled in the cities and among the educated, is to socially identify them with their father and not with their maternal uncles.

Earlier spatially close frequency of social contacts was regular. Change of residence from rural to urban setting and change of occupational pattern caused for the changes in interactional pattern as well. Social interaction is evidenced in the major areas of deaths, engagements, marriages and births. Among the Christian Khasis, as the traditional rites are not practised as vigorously as earlier, interaction is also cut down in this area as well.

The Khasi community is more flexible and accommodative compared to the other matrilineal communities, like Nairs. In the case of Nairs, marriage by a woman with a low caste man or begetting a child from a member of low caste was considered as great sin and the culprits were summarily out casted from the community and even performed her death rituals as it is in the case of real dead. Even though a Nair woman could marry a Nambudiri man who is considered to be superior in the local caste hierarchy (hypergamous marriages), marriage with a low caste man was strictly prohibited. In the case of Khasis, though they discouraged marriage with a non-Khasi man or woman, once married they accommodated them in the community. Even though the descent is reckoned strictly through female line they have developed their own mechanisms to accommodate the children born to Khasi man in a relationship with a non-Khasi woman in their community by originating new clans. In that respect the Khasi community was more accommodative and flexible compared to many other matrilineal communities in the country.

In the present day Khasi society, the male members are physically unavailable to his own matrilineal descent group due to the matrilocal pattern of residence. Traditionally this problem was solved by the custom of village endogamous marriages so that his accessibility to his own descent group is not a problem. Now a days, due to the spatial mobility of a Khasi due to education and occupation this proximity was cut down to a considerable extent. A man is thus gradually alienated from his own descent group. Due to his emotional attachment to his children and wife and also due to the pattern of matrilocal residence he weans away from his own and assimilates himself with his wife's descent group. The degree of alienation from his own group and assimilation with his wife's descent group have great repercussions as it will disturb the continuity of the matrilineal descent group and the continuity of the matrilineal system itself.

The community is gradually moving to an equigeniture mode of succession and inheritance pattern. Many parents in the urban settings are found giving a share of their property to their destitute sons and daughters other than the youngest. But still the family house and a major share of their property are maintained by the *khadduh* herself. In many cases the sons are found building houses in the land provided by his parents and their wives joining them in that household. Thus locality patterns are also gradually shifting from matrilocal or *matri-neolocal* to a '*patri-neolocal*' pattern. There are many other reasons as well for this shift in the locality patterns in the Sawmer village (one of the two villages selected for this study). Most of the people in this village are government servants working in the offices located in and around Shillong town. In cases, if their spouses are from villages (interestingly the spouses in most cases are from the Cherra area), it is impossible for them to live matrilocally as they cannot leave Shillong since they are working there. In such cases the most practical solution to the problem is to live neolocally in the husband's village. The Khadduh sister generally cannot make any objections if the parents part with a portion of their property to their sons as they can sell the property if they so wish and if she makes any objections they can show that it is only a sale but not inheritance of family property.

Another reason for this shift is that the institution of *ka khadduh* is becoming increasingly vulnerable and many boys feel as "outsider" in their own house. 'Money matters not the custom' was the reaction of some. It is the experience of this situation prompted many parents to think that their sons and elder daughters also should get something from their property or savings.

The real situation in the villages studied differs basically in some aspects. Nongrem is a more or less traditional village observing most of their traditional practices steadfastly. But in Sawmer, since it is in a semi-urban setting they gradually discard some aspects of their traditional culture. In Nongrem if the husband purchases some land with his hard-earned money they always get it registered in the name of their wives but in Sawmer, the practice now is not like that and they buy it in their own name. They believe that there is no question of alienating the land since it will go only to their own children and not to his nephews and nieces as in olden days.

Traditionally, the Khasi men are close to their mother, sister and the sisters' children and the maternal uncles have been given much importance. But now a days, for the fathers their sisters and the sisters' children are of secondary considerations, and they are more akin to their wives and children. They themselves get involved in the family matters of their sisters whenever a situation of urgency of that sort arises. The *ka khadduh* normally consults his brothers or uncles before the sale of property of the *iing* (the Khasi domestic unit) as a matter of formality and to keep them in good terms and to maintain the family cohesion. The relationship between husband and brothers in-law varies from family to family but in general they try to maintain the relationship in a cordial way as far as possible.

The Khasis always prefer a female child as the family continues only through her but they never shows any step motherly attitude towards their male children on that ground. But most of the mothers shared the view that the boys will go and stay with their in-laws after getting married and their daughters only look after them in their old age and hence they should be given priorities.

In the extended families of the *khadduh,* if her parents are still able enough to manage the household things they wield the authority; mother manages the day-to-day affairs of the family in consultation with her husband. If they are aged, the *khadduh* and her husband look after the day-to-day affairs of the family. All other matters which are of wider applications concerning the whole *iing*, she has to be consulted her maternal uncle and in his absence, her eldest brother. In the houses of the *khadduh* the visits of her maternal uncles or brothers will be regular and it will be more frequent if the mother of the *khadduh* is alive.

The nuclear family comprises the husband, wife and their unmarried children. In such houses the visits of wife's brothers or maternal uncles may not be as frequent as it is in *khadduh's* house. In the nuclear families the mother is the manager of the family. She procures all the household items and the husbands generally entrust their income to her to manage the family in consultation with her husband and the male members generally will not involve by themselves in such matters. The male children's earnings are to be given to the mother and they use it for day-to-day expenses or they may accumulate it to purchase some landed property. After marriage he will entrust his earnings to his wife and his mother has no say over it. A property, which is landed in character, secured by a male member with his hard-earned money, is always getting registered in the name of his wife. This will ward off the danger of going the property to his maternal relatives on his death.

If the mother of the *khadduh* is alive and wielding authority in the family, the frequency of visits by the brothers would be more frequent and enjoy more importance, freedom and say in the family matters. In that case they will have a more emotional relationship with their *iing.* If one gets divorced he has no other option but to return to his original family where his sister has already established a family of her own. If the mother is alive he may not be facing much difficulty but in her absence he may not be feeling as comfortable as earlier when his mother was alive.

Now a days the children are found more attached to their fathers than to their maternal uncles. In everyday activities the maternal uncles never interfere and their relation with their nephews and nieces is more formal than that of an intimate one. If the maternal uncles are living in some other villages with his own wife and children they normally do not get much time to visit his sisters and their children as frequently as he wishes. The maternal uncles will be consulted on all-important occasions and matters relating to *iing* but the day-to-day affairs of the family will be discussed and settled within the family itself. The nephews and nieces respect and revere their maternal uncles, keep a distance with them and do not mingle with them as freely as it is with their father. This difference in the behavioural pattern shows that they still venerate the authority held by their maternal uncles but that they are emotionally more attached to their father.

The father in the modern context find himself confronted with new roles and duties to perform with a greater responsibility to shoulder than in the past. In the past the role of the father was limited to that of the breadwinner. He took care of the small domestic problems that may arise. He even assisted the management of his wife's ancestral property. Now as the sphere of day-to-day life widens the involvement of fathers in the activities of the family especially those pertaining to the children are also widens. As the spheres of duties to be performed were limited in the traditional way of life, the duties and responsibilities of the father and the maternal uncles were not precisely defined. The father had only a limited role to perform in a family. The elder males' responsibilities were more of religious and social nature and the maternal uncle usually met them. Today what is expected to be delivered to the youngsters is more than the religious and social but they have to take care of their education, socialisation, career, food and clothing and a lot other that the modern world demands. In all these spheres of life the maternal and paternal responsibilities are not so defined and the fathers' involvement is more visible. Thus when the responsibility of a Khasi man as a maternal uncle dwindles the responsibility as a father is on increase. Nevertheless in decision regarding the sale of ancestral property and in disputes among siblings, the maternal uncle has not lost his influence.

*****

A Khasi man in his traditional dancing dress during Seng kut Snem

A Khasi man blowing the tangmuri (flute)

Eucharist Day Procession at Shillong

Eucharist Day Procession- Women in their traditional attire

A Khasi woman

Chapter - VI

Concluding Remarks

Matrilineal systems in its traditional form are hardly in existence anywhere in the world. Matrilineal descent groups gradually disintegrate under economic changes brought about by contact with western industrial nations (Gough, 1961:631). Fortes (1949:60-61) sees that unstable social system produced by occupational differentiation, stratification by income, education and rank, geographical and social mobility, as well as disparate values in religious beliefs are root causes for the disintegration of matrilineal systems. Economic changes brought about by changes in production relations, because of culture contacts, tempt communities like Rabhas to choose the path of change (Raha 1989). Introduction of cash crop farming and subsequent economic changes have brought radical kinship changes among many matrilineal communities like Tonga, Ndembu, Yao, Ashanthi and Nayar (Colson, 1961, Turner, 1957, Mitchell, 1956, Fortes, 1949, Gough: 1961).

The Khasi society is not immune to the types of changes that are taking place among matrilineal societies the world over. However, the process and direction of changes are different. An alternative value system is gradually emerging putting tremendous pressure on the matrilineal systems in that society and this shift is not due to a 'single factor', but is a cumulative outcome of a wide variety of factors evident in that society today. Though the impingement has been considerable in some areas, in many other respects, their traditional mores have remained unaffected.

The Khasis still follow the matrilineal system of descent and inheritance. But elements of changes are visible in several aspects of their culture, which survive around the matrilineal system. The close link of matrilineal system with their traditional religion helped them to restrain change to a great extent. The Khasis have been a tradition-bound society. It often persuaded its members to cling on to their old age customs and traditions by enforcing various kinds of sanctions on deviants. In a close-knit society no one can live as a social isolate and hence they observed the traditional norms and values as strictly as possible.

Several extraneous elements are gradually penetrating in the social self of the community. Some elements like Christianity, with a strong patrilineal bias, have already made deep inroads in their socio-religious life. Those who embraced Christianity began to neglect many of their customs and practises and rites and rituals without observing them as strictly as earlier. Christianity often prefers the paternal to maternal involvements in their socio-religious observances. The modern transport and communication facilities have helped them to shift from traditional subsistence based agricultural productions to cash crops. This shift in their production pattern introduced them to a commercial economy bringing tremendous changes in their lifestyles. As a result, the little stratified Khasi society emerges as a stratified society based on property and income. A middle class based on economic prosperity is gradually emerging among them. In such a society negative sanctions by the community against the deviants seldom works and it ultimately affects the continuity of the matrilineal system itself.

The spread of modern education also affected the matrilineal system in several ways. Modern education has helped them in finding lucrative jobs in Government services and in other fields. This has brought spatial and occupational mobility making them unable to perform their traditional duties as strictly as demanded by the matrilineal system. The modern world demands much of the parental attention in the affairs of their children limiting the scope for their involvement in the affairs of their sisters, nephews and nieces and thus giving a twist to the traditional authority structures. The social conditions in Khasi society today are indicative of functional adjustment to the changing male roles in that society.

Adoption of Christian faith, spread of education, introduction to commercial economy, enrolment in Government service, etc, have brought them in contact with other cultures. Among the youth there is a growing tendency to imbibe more and more elements from other cultures and to neglect their own.

The present study submits that some kind of stress and strain is evident in that society and witness a decreasing influence of the matrilineal group on its members, because of many factors like spread of education, urbanization, etc. What is observable today in Khasi matriliny is a painful transition and change. Matriliny creates a very feeling of inferiority and insecurity in the male from the very beginning and cause for set in frustration and it makes them grow irresponsible. Aberrations arise within the matrilineal system mostly due to the change in value systems and the consciousness of its members on the materialistic side of the system in the changed social scenario.

The present study has some inputs to show that the matrilineal system prevalent among the Khasis has its impact on the process of personality formation of the Khasi youth and that the female children are receiving some preferential treatment in the family owing to the matrilineal system but its impact on the Khasi men needs to be assessed using psychological techniques. The frustration the young men suffers in the society is the cumulative outcome of a wide variety of factors the youths are facing the world over and not merely the result of one particular system, but the matrilineal system has its own contribution in compounding the already set in anxieties. The matrilineal system, though offers a lot of social and economic leverages to the women folk, its position in the Khasi society is not of absolute authority and power. The women today are subjected to a lot of social evils such as harassment from husbands, frequent divorces, single parenting of children, etc., and its magnitude is on the increase day by day.

In the present day Khasi society the whole fabric of matrilineal system is facing challenges of change from various quarters and as a result is evolving certain social mechanisms that will help to maintain, adopt, adjust, and that will ensure the survival and continuity of the society. There may not be any sudden changes as far as the descent and kinship patterns are concerned but changes could already been observed as far as inheritance, succession, authority and residence pattern, decision making, etc., are concerned.

*****

Khasi men in their traditional dancing dress during Seng kut Snem

Khasi men with their musical instruments

Khasi women in their Traditional wear

Procession during Seng Kut Snem

Seng Kut Snem festival of Khasis

Seng Kut Snem Festival

References

Aiyappan, A and Mahadevan, K. 1990. *Ecology, Economy, Matrilliny and Fertility of Kurichias*. New Delhi: B.R. publications.

Bareh, Hamlet. 1967. *The History and Culture of the Khasi People*. Guwahati: Spectrum Publications.

Briffault, Robert. 1927. *The Mothers* Vol.I. New York: The Macmillan Company.

Cantile, K. 1934. *Notes on Khasi Law*. Abardeen.

Challam, Margaret B (Ed.) 1999. *The Dynamics of Family System in a Matriliny of Meghalaya*. Shillong: Tribal Research Institute.

Chaudhuri, Sarit 1994. "The Lalung" in *The People of India- Meghalaya.* Calcutta: Anthropological Survey of India.

Cherian, P.J. 1999. *Cultural formation of Kerala.* Thiruvananthapuram: Kerala State Gazetteers Department.

Chhakchhuak, Linda. 2005. "Meghalaya Protects Matriliny" in The Meghalaya Guardian (Daily) 7th July, 2005.

Chow... ...996. *The Khasi People*. Shillong.

Clatterbaugh. 1990. Contemporary perspectives on Masculinity.Boulder: Westview.

Colson, E. 1961. "Plateau Tonga" in Schneider, D.M and K.Gough(Eds) *Matrilineal Kinship*. Berkeley: University of California Press.

Dkhar, Aibor 2004. "Do women really enjoy privileged status in Matrilineal Meghalaya" in The Sentinel (Daily), 18th August, 2004.

Das, Manosh 2005. "Child Trafficking worry over Meghalaya" in Hindustan Times (Daily), 2nd April, 2005.

Driver, Harold E. 1997. "Cross Cultural Studies" in JJ Honigman (Ed) Handbook of social and cultural anthropology Vol-I Jaipur: Rawat Publications.

Dube, Leela. 1997. *Women and Kinship: Comparative Perspectives on Gender in South and South East Asia*. New Delhi: Vistar Publications.

Du Bois, Cora. 1960. *Lowie's Selected Papers in Anthropology*. Berkeley: University of California Press.

Ehrenfels, Baron Von. 1941. *Mother right in India*. Oxford University Press.

Fortes, M. 1949. "Time and Social Structure : An Ashanti Case study". In Fred Eggan and Meyer Fortes (Eds) Social Structure. London: Oxford University Press.

Friend, Pereira. 1912. "The Rabhas" in *Census of Assam 1911, Vol.III, Part*-I Report

Fuller, C.J. 1976. *The Nayars Today*. Cambridge: Cambridge University Press.

Gabrielle, Bertrand. 1958. *Secret Lands where women reign.*

Gassah, L.S. 1999. "Review of the views on matrilineal system among the Khasi-Jaintia people" in Challam, Margaret B (Ed.) *The Dynamics of Family System in a Matriliny of Meghalaya*. Shillong: Tribal Research Institute.

Gopinathan Nair. 1983. *Asian Migration to the Middle East: Emigration from India.* Working paper No.180, Thiruvananthapuram: Centre for Development Studies.

Goswami, B.B. 1979. *Cultural Profile of Shillong*. Kolkata: Anthropological Survey of India.

Gourdon, P.R.T. 1975 (Reprint). *The Khasis*.Delhi: Cosmos Publications.

Gassah (Ed).1997. *The Autonomous District Councils*. New Delhi: Omsons Publications.

Hans- Dieter Evers. 1974. "Changing pattern of Minangkabau Land ownership" working Paper No.22. University of Singapore.

Honigmann, J. J. Ed.1997. *Handbook of Social and Cultural Anthropology.* Jaipur: Rawat Publications.

Joshi, SC. 2005. "Status of children with special reference to Nothr-East" in The Assam Tribunal (Daily) 1st and 2nd February, 2005.

Khongphai. 1979. "Seng Khasi" in B.B.Goswami.(Ed.) *Cultural Profile of Shillong.* Calcutta: Anthropological Survey of India.

Kluckhohn, Clyde.1962. *Culture and Behaviour*. The Free Press.

Krishna Iyer, L. A 1995. "Degeneration of Matriliny" in LK Balaratnam(Ed.) *Man in Kerala*. Palghat: Centram Publications.

Lakiang, PK. 1999. "Ka Seng (taboo) in the context of kur (clan) relation" in Challam, Margaret B (Ed.) *The Dynamics of Family System in a Matriliny of 9Meghalaya.* Shillong: Tribal Research Institute.

Lakshmanan, C. 2004. "Dalit Masculinities in Social Science Research" in EPW, March- 6, 2004.

Lowie. 1960. "Social Organization" in Cora Du Bois(Ed.) *Lowie's Selected Papers in Anthropology.* Berkeley: University of California Press.

Lyngdoh, J. Darningstone. 2005. "State women commission" in Meghalaya Gurdian (Daily) 8th March, 2005.

Lyngdoh, MPR. 1999. "Inheritance, Property rights and entrepreneurship in the Khasi society" in Challam, Margaret B (Ed.) *The Dynamics of Family System in a Matriliny of Meghalaya*. Shillong: Tribal Research Institute.

Lyngdoh, SS. 1999. "Breakdown of authority and discipline in the Hynniewtrep present family setup" in Challam, Margaret B (Ed.) *The Dynamics of Family System in a Matriliny of Meghalaya.* Shillong: Tribal Research Institute.

Mac Innes. 1998. *The End of Masculinity.* Bukingham: Open University Press.

Majumdar, DN. 1978. *Culture change in two Garo villages*. Calcutta: Anthropological Survey of India.

Malngiang, Pascal. 1999. "A critique of the Khasi Matriliny" in Challam, Margaret B (Ed.) *The Dynamics of Family System in a Matriliny of Meghalaya.* Shillong: Tribal Research Institute.

Mathur P.R.G. 1979. *The Khasis of Meghalaya*. New Delhi: Cosmo Publications.

Menon, T.M. 2002. *A Handbook of Kerala.* Thiruvananthapuram: International School of Dravidian Linguistics.

Mitchell, J. Clyde. 1956. *The Yao Village*. Manchester: Manchester University Press.

Morgan, D.H.G. 1992. *Discovering Men*. London: Routledge.

Mukhim, Patricia. 1999. "Crisis of Authority in the Khasi Matrilineal society" in Challam, Margaret B (Ed.) *The Dynamics of Family System in a Matriliny of Meghalaya*. Shillong: Tribal Research Institute.

Mukhim, Patricia. 2002a. "The Khasi Worldview" in *Shillong Times* (Daily), 2nd August 2002.

Mukhim, Patricia. 2002b. "Old wine, New bottle" in The Telegraph, North East (Daily) 24th September, 2002.

Mukhim, Patricia. 2003. "Traditional Institutions-a critique" in *Shillong Times* (Daily), 3rd October, 2003.

Mukhim, Patricia. 2004. "A Myth called Matriliny" in Telegraph;13th January,2004.

Nakane, Chie. 1961. *Garo and Khasi: A comparative Study in Matrilineal System,* Hague: Mouton and Co.

Natarajan, N. 1982. "Cultural Revivalism among the Christian Khasis of Meghalaya" in *Tribal movements in India*, Singh K.S. New Delhi: Manohar Publications.

Passah, Philomath. 1999. "Impediments to entrepreneurship in Matrilineal societies of Meghalaya" in Challam, Margaret B (Ed.) *The Dynamics of Family System in a Matriliny of Meghalaya*. Shillong: Tribal Research Institute.

Raha, M.K. 1989. *Matriliny to Patriliny: A Study of the Rabha Society*. New Delhi: Gian Publishung House.

Ranjini, D. 2000. *Nayar Women Today*. New Delhi: Classical Publishing Company.

Richards, A.I. 1950. "Some types of family Structure amongst the Central Bantu" in A.R. Radcliff Brown and C.D.Forde (Eds) *African System of Kinship and marriage*; London: Oxford university Press.

Roy, j. 1897. *Ka Niam Jong Ki Khasi.*

Rynjah, S. 1999. "The Khasi family- Dynamic role of father and maternal uncle" in Challam, Margaret B (Ed.) *The Dynamics of Family System in a Matriliny of Meghalaya*. Shillong: Tribal Research Institute.

Sarma, S. 2003. *Meghalaya: The Land and Forest*. Guwahati: Geophil Publishing House.

Sasikumar. M. 1996. "The Kurichias" in Menon and Sasikumar (Eds). *Encyclopaedia of Dravidian Tribes Vol-II.* Trivandrum: International School of Dravidian Linguistics.

Sasikumar. M. 1999. *Arumbukuttam Vellalas of Tamil Nadu*. Unpublished Report.

Sasikumar.M. 2005. "Changing power structure in a Matrilineal society: A case study of Khasis" in AK Ray and RP Athparia (Eds) *Women and Changing power structure in North east India*. New Delhi: Om Publications.

Schneider, David.M and K.Gough. 1961. *Matrilineal Kinship*. Berkeley: University of California Press.

Sedgwick, E.K. 1985. *Between Men: English literature and male Homo social Desire*. New York: Colombia University Press.

Saradamony, K. 1991. *Matriliny Transformed*. New Delhi: Sage Publications.

Shadap- Sen, N.C. 1981. *The origin and early history of the Khasi-Synteng People*. Calcutta: Firma Klm Private Limited.

Syiem, IM. 1999. "Khasi Matriliny in Transition" in Challam, Margaret B(Ed.) *The Dynamics of Family System in a Matriliny of Meghalaya*. Shillong: Tribal Research Institute.

Tiwari, B.K, et al. 1999. *Sacred Forests of Meghalaya*. Shillong: Regional Centre: National Afforestation and Eco-Development Board, North Eastern Hill University.

Thurston, E. 1975(Reprint). *The Castes and Tribes of Southern India*. Delhi: Cosmos Publications.

Unny, Govindan. 1994. *Kinship Systems in South and South East Asia*. New Delhi: Vikas Publishing House Pvt. Ltd.

Turner, V.W. 1957. *Schism and Continuity in an African Society*. Manchester: Manchester University Press.

Wolflang, C. 1999. "Property rights and entrepreneurship in a Matriliny" in Challam, Margaret B (Ed.) *The Dynamics of Family System in a Matriliny of Meghalaya*. Shillong: Tribal Research Institute.

Meghalaya Guardian (Daily) 26th June, 2004. "Illicit Trafficking in Meghalaya".

The Sentinel (Daily) 29th March, 2004. "Female sex ratio up in Meghalaya". Shillong Times (Daily) 2nd February, 2005.

*****

Index